CHACS AND CHIEFS

THE ICONOLOGY OF MOSAIC STONE SCULPTURE IN PRE-CONQUEST YUCATÁN, MEXICO

ROSEMARY SHARP

Dumbarton Oaks   Trustees for Harvard University   Washington, D.C. 1981

ACKNOWLEDGMENTS

This monograph was begun when George Kubler invited me to come to Yale as a Visiting Fellow in the Department of the History of Art in the Fall of 1974. It was continued while I was a Research Scholar at Dumbarton Oaks under a Robert Woods Bliss Postdoctoral Fellowship during the Spring of 1975. It was completed under the guidance of Gordon Willey during my appointment as a Research Fellow and Lecturer in the Harvard Department of Anthropology and the Peabody Museum from 1976–1978, with financial assistance from a Postdoctoral Research Fellowship from the American Council of Learned Societies.

I am deeply grateful to George Kubler, Tatiana Proskouriakoff, and Gordon Willey for their continued advice, encouragement, and support in the preparation and publication of this manuscript.

I am also indebted to Elizabeth Boone and Blenda Femenias for their careful editing, scrutiny, and presentation of the manuscript to the printers.

There are many friends, colleagues, teachers, and other special people who have contributed in various valuable ways to the completion of this monograph. I want to thank especially Marie Jeanne Adams, Ann Blalock, Edward Bodner, Carol Jopling, Eugenia Kaledin, Isabelle and Arden King, Dorothy Lofdahl, Martha and Donald Robertson, Rachel Stewart, and Irvin Taube, and, above all, my children, Lesley, Paula, and Erik.

Library of Congress Cataloging in Publication Data

Sharp, Rosemary, 1929–
Chacs and chiefs.
(Studies in pre-Columbian art and archaeology; no. 24)
Bibliography: p. 42.
1. Mayas—Sculpture. 2. Mayas—Tribal government.
3. Indians of Mexico—Yucatan—Sculpture. 4. Indians
of Mexico—Yucatan—Tribal government. 5. Mayas—
Religion and mythology. 6. Indians of Mexico—
Yucatan—Religion and mythology. I. Title. II. Series.
E51.S85   no. 24   [F1435.3.S34]   970s [730′.972′65]
ISBN 0-88402-099-1   80-26269

Introduction

Art forms and styles supply us with a major source of information about past civilizations, especially those for which we have no contemporary and generally understood written documents. Archaeologists concerned with Middle American problems are now devoting progressively more attention to qualitative cultural aspects in addition to the material and measurable ones. In their studies they are considering the connections between ideology and other facets of culture and are investigating the ways in which visual arts articulate with political, economic, social, and other systems.[1]

How do artistic systems relate to other cultural systems? The techniques of both the anthropologist and the historian of art have been brought to bear on this problem. Previous analyses[2] indicate that the method for solving it involves consideration of critical motifs and patterns, their visual and archaeological contexts, the manner in which these elements cluster in time and space, and their meanings in specific historical situations.

With these factors in mind, I will attempt here to relate a unique form of architectural decoration from Pre-Hispanic Yucatán, Mexico, to ideological and political systems in that area. I will also postulate that this art form served both as a mediating system between cosmology and politics—between Chacs and chiefs—and as a visual manifestation of a dynamic compromise which was made in a time of transition.

An Inter-regional Style of the Epiclassic Period

Many of the major public buildings at such sites as Chichén Itzá on the Northern Plains, and Uxmal, Labná, Sayil, and Kabah in the Puuc Hill area of Yucatán (Fig. 1), from the period referred to here as "Epiclassic,"[3] are decorated with mosaic stone sculpture (Fig. 2). This artistic manifestation represented one aspect of an inter-regional style, present also in the Valley of Oaxaca, at such sites as Monte Albán, Atzompa, Lambityeco, Yagul, and Mitla, and at El Tajín in Veracruz (Sharp 1970, 1978, n.d.a).

The Epiclassic Period begins, very roughly, at about A.D. 650–750, approximately the time of the fall of Teotihuacan in Central Mexico, and ends at about A.D. 950–1000, the time when Puuc centers in northwestern Yucatán are thought to have been

---

[1] For studies involving ideology, see Haviland (1975, 1978) and Willey (1962; 1973: 161; 1976; 1977: 416–417); for studies involving the visual arts, see Coe (1972), Flannery and Marcus (1976), Ingham (1971: 625–626), C. Millon (1973), Puleston (1977), and Sharp (1978, n.d.a, n.d.b, n.d.c, n.d.d).

[2] For discussions of methodologies and interpretations of Pre-Hispanic Middle American iconography, see Grieder (1975: 849–855), Kubler (1973: 163–167; 1975a: 757–767), Nicholson (1976: 157–175), and Willey (1973: 153–162).

[3] "Epiclassic" is a term that was first used by Wigberto Jiménez Moreno (1966: 42, 47, 64) to refer to a period extending roughly from A.D. 650 to 1000, or to the final part of the Classic horizon; see also Paddock (1966: 233–234) and Webb (1978).

abandoned. It overlaps temporally, at one end, with the terminal stage of southern Classic Maya civilization, and, at the other, with the Toltec manifestation at Chichén Itzá.[4] It was a period of crisis and rapid change, an era of reformulation of ways of life and world views, and a time in which power was redefined, redesigned, and reassigned.

The periodization of Pre-Hispanic Middle American history, the placement of its boundaries, and the naming of its parts represent a major theoretical problem, one that goes beyond the scope of this paper.[5] The term "Epiclassic" is used predominantly here, rather than the more generally accepted "Terminal Classic," to stress the fact that we are concerned most in this study with a *transitional* manifestation of *inter-regional* scope, with an horizon with its own characteristics (Sharp 1970, 1978; Webb 1978), rather than with the final phase of a regional tradition. "Terminal Classic" has been limited here to the discussion of characteristics at sites in the southern Maya lowlands (Fig. 1), which were partly contemporaneous with Epiclassic phenomena, but which differed from these in significant ways (see, e.g., Ball 1974: 86; Webb 1978).

Unfortunately, the term "Epiclassic" implies that something culturally old is on its way out, whereas the more crucial aspect of this period, in my opinion, involves new patterns which are taking shape. A better, but more awkward, term would be "Pro-topostclassic" (Davies 1977: 76), or even "Prepostclassic." The conventional term has been used here, however, to avoid adding more confusion to what is already a terminological snarl.

The mosaic stone sculpture that serves as an important diagnostic for the Epiclassic Period is composed of pieces of carved and shaped stones of standard sizes and forms (Fig. 3).[6] These were assembled into geometric motifs and patterns, and tenoned into the façades of monumental public buildings and elite tombs. The patterns produced are characterized by simplicity, repetition, and symmetry (Fig. 4).

Amid these patterns, naturalistic representations are almost nonexistent in Oaxaca and Veracruz. They are also rare in Yucatán, being limited for the most part in this area to such ornaments as small huts (Fig. 5), warriors, floral designs, serpents, and miniature human heads.[7]

Of the motifs involved, the simpler T and stepfret, and the composite mask are particularly important for understanding the iconography of power during the Epiclassic Period in northern Yucatán. All three have reasonable time depth, appearing in one medium or another during the Classic Period (*ca.* A.D. 250–900). They cluster together at sites in both Oaxaca and Yucatán, and their possible meanings in various contexts have been carefully considered by a number of scholars.

---

[4] For a discussion of the "collapse" of Teotihuacan, see R. Millon (1973: 60–61); for end dates of the Classic Period in Oaxaca, see Rabin (1970); for the chronology of El Tajín, Veracruz, see García Payón (1971: Table 1). Rands (1973: 35, 38) suggests that the collapse of the Classic Maya site of Palenque, for example, probably occurred between A.D. 800 and 830. According to Diehl and Benfer (1975: 117), the earliest definite settlement at Tula, Hidalgo, occurred about the same time, and its major period of growth took place from about A.D. 900 to 1000; see also Diehl (1974: 190). Andrews V (1979: 8) calls attention to the overlap of Pure and Modified Florescent Periods (Epiclassic and Postclassic Periods) in northern Yucatán.

[5] For a discussion of problems of periodization, and of patterns and processes of the Epiclassic Period, see Paddock (1966: 111–112) and Webb (1978); of the Terminal Classic Maya era, see Willey and Shimkin (1973: 457–501) and Willey (1977: 406–407).

[6] Mosaic stone sculpture has traditionally been referred to in English and Spanish as *greca*, and in French as *greque*, since long ago everything found in the New World was being conceived of in Old World terms, and the geometric forms of this Pre-Hispanic sculpture resembled the Greek meander (see Sharp 1970). "Greca" is also used by American archaeologists to refer to particular geometric motifs, e.g., the step-fret, in other media, whether presented singly or in series. Because of this broad application, and the Old World overtones, the term has been avoided in this paper.

[7] The Palace of the Governors, Uxmal, apparently had some representations approaching portraiture. It is not known when they were applied to the buildings. Moreover, they would have been recessive, as small objects against the mosaic background. See Foncerrada de Molina (1965: Fig. 31) for an illustration.

The T

The T or Tau is a common motif in Central and Southern Mexico, and in the Maya area. It appears both right-side-up and in inverted form, but the extent to which such distinctions may indicate differences in meanings is not known.[8] It is usually found in sequence and often in association with the step-fret or the mask, or both (Figs. 6, 13).

In Oaxaca, sequences of Ts appear with scroll forms, and sequences of step-pyramids (a similar and probably closely related form) occur with step-frets on elite pottery from Late Preclassic to Early Classic times (Fig. 7) (Monte Albán II, *ca*. 100 B.C.–A.D. 250; Winter, Gaxiola, and Alaniz 1975: Table). Ts also appear during the Middle and Late Classic and Epiclassic Periods (Monte Albán III-A, III-B, *ca*. A.D. 250–650) on pottery urns. For example, in Figure 8, T-sequences frame the masked face of Cocijo, generally considered by scholars to be the Zapotec "rain god."[9]

In addition, it is one of the earliest motifs set into stone mosaic patterns in this area, where it is used in inverted form to decorate the lower part of platforms both at Monte Albán and at Yagul during Classic and Epiclassic times.[10] Sequences of inverted Ts occur also at Lambityeco, primarily an Epiclassic site, again in association with Cocijo masks, and near the major pyramid at the site which is decorated with sequences of step-frets (Figs. 9, 25). Possibly the most magnificent T in this region, however, is that first mentioned by Désiré Charnay, an

early traveler. Charnay (1888: 501) observed that at Mitla "the great palace . . . consists of a vast edifice in the shape of a Tau."

In Central Mexico, at Teotihuacan, the major Classic urban site of the area, sequences of inverted Ts are used as crenelations on the roofs of temples and elite houses (Sejourné 1966: Lám. XCI). Sequences of step-pyramids, each having a square or rectangular basal notch, are used in the same manner both in pictorial representations (Fig. 10) and on actual buildings (Sejourné 1966: Lám. LXXXIII). At Cholula, Puebla, to the east, T-sequences are utilized as a dominant decorative feature, embellishing slightly concave *taluds* (sloping ramps) on major pyramidal structures (Fig. 11). Moreover, one of the smaller platforms at this site is also T-shaped.

To the north, at El Tajín, Veracruz, inverted Ts and step-pyramids (with basal notches) appear also as crenelations on carved reliefs in the South Ball Court, Panels 5 and 6 (Kampen 1972: Figs. 24, 25). In addition, at the Mound of the Building Columns, step-pyramids occur in a manner reminiscent of the Oaxaca urn in Figure 8, as a framing device around an important figure, in this case, one seated on a platform decorated with step-frets (Fig. 12) (Kampen 1972: Fig. 32b).

The T was common also in both southern Classic Maya and northern Yucatecan contexts. It is the identifying element of the day-sign "Ik," a term meaning "wind," "breath," "spirit," and, by extension, "life" (Thompson 1970a: 257; Proskouriakoff 1974: 159). Moreover, it is one of the important components of the glyph for Schellhas' God B, the Maya "rain god" (Fig. 36c) (T-668; Thompson 1962: 264), which occurs in the codices from this area, and at Chichén Itzá and Uxmal (Thompson 1970a: 257). (See also note 26.)

The T is also used to trim the garments of noble figures, as on Relief Panel 2, probably from Palenque, Chiapas (Coe and Benson 1966: Fig. 6), now in the Dumbarton Oaks collection. It is found, too, on plaques and ornaments taken from the sacred *cenote* (or natural well), Chichén Itzá (Proskouriakoff 1974: 159), a place of pilgrimage and human

---

[8] For example, the T appears right-side-up both in northern Yucatán (Figs. 6, 15) and in Central Mexico at Cholula, Puebla (Fig. 11). Inverted Ts occur at Monte Albán, and at Lambityeco and Yagul in Oaxaca (Sharp 1970: Figs. 14, 19).

[9] For a discussion of Monte Albán II in relation to "Classic" Mesoamerica, see Paddock 1966: 111–112; see also Paddock 1978: 53. For identification and discussion of Cocijo, see Caso and Bernal (1952: 17–49), Paddock (1966: 128, 138), and Seler (1904: 267–301). For an interesting opposing view related to the problem of supernatural figures and religion in Pre-Hispanic Middle America in general, see Hvidtfeldt (1958).

[10] Inverted Ts appear within a tablero on a building in the interior of the North Platform, Monte Albán, Monte Albán IIIb, and on the platform in Patio 4, Yagul (Sharp 1970: Fig. 19).

sacrifice (Tozzer 1957). In addition, a pair of T motifs is displayed in association with opposing step-frets on the Palace at Palenque, from the latter part of the Classic Period (Fig. 14). Finally, Tatiana Proskouriakoff (1974: 159) notes that Tau symbols are also to be found worn as pectorals "by figures on the sides of the sarcophagus in the tomb beneath the Temple of the Inscriptions . . . [at Palenque], by a figure on Altar Q at Copán, and by small dwarf figures on stelae of Caracol."

In northern Yucatán, stone mosaics also serve as media for this motif. It is usually found here in association with long-nosed masks, as on the Palace at Labná (Figs. 6, 15), and it occurs clustered with masks and step-frets on the East Annex of the Monjas (Nunnery), Chichén Itzá (Fig. 13).

To summarize, the T adorns pottery, platforms, palaces, temples, pyramids, and murals. Even major and minor buildings appear to have been constructed with this shape in mind. It is associated during the Classic and Epiclassic Periods with step-frets, and with a masked figure interpreted as a "rain god." It is found in an elite context. Finally, in Maya iconography, at least, it signifies the wind and breath, and qualities such as spirit and life itself.

The Step-fret

The step-fret, like the T, is an old motif in Pre-Hispanic Middle American iconography.[11] It ornaments pottery, painted murals, gold objects, manuscripts, stone reliefs, and masks, as well as the exteriors of buildings. Because it is such a common image, as with the first motif, only a limited number of examples will be supplied here to suggest its range, associations, meanings, and general importance.

Pottery and Paintings

It appears first in Middle America in Oaxaca during Monte Albán II times on polychrome and bichrome pottery found in elite tombs (Caso, Bernal, and Acosta 1967: Lám. IVa, c; Lám. x). As noted earlier, it occurs in association with the step-pyramid (Fig. 7). It is used later to decorate the elaborate garments of certain supernaturals, human celebrants, priests, or god impersonators who are shown on the walls of Tomb 105 walking in single file (Fig. 16) (Monte Albán IIIb?; Kubler 1975b: 97; 350, fn. 16).[12]

Step-frets are found also in several painted murals at Teotihuacan from Middle to Late Classic times. For example, at the Palace of the Sun, step-frets decorate the dorsal area of what appears to be a jaguar-serpent-bird (Fig. 17). At the Palace of the Quetzal Butterfly, sequences of step-frets with equivalent ground-figure patterns are painted on the dado of the patio (Fig. 18). Carved stone piers in this patio are embellished with owl-serpents and quetzal-birds, which George Kubler (1967: 10) interprets as having "connected meanings probably pertaining to war and a named dynasty."[13]

Within the Maya area, step-frets are particularly common during the Terminal Classic Period in the Usumacinta River area. For example, at Bonam-

[11] The step-fret motif, however, occurs earlier in Peru than in Middle America. For example, it is present on a fragment of pottery taken from the Temple of Chavín de Huantar (Tello 1960: 350, Fig. 174, bottom, far right) dating to the Chavín Period. The earliest radiocarbon dates for Chavín culture are 1190±60 B.C., 1360±80 B.C., 1730±80 B.C. (Pozorski 1975: 247–248). Chavín extends to about 200–100 B.C. (Rowe and Menzel 1967: Chronology Table of Peruvian Coast; Lumbreras 1974: 57–80).

[12] Caso (1938; 1965: 864–865) calls these figures "gods" and "goddesses." Their profile positions, however, suggest that they may be human beings playing various ritualistic roles. For an application of positional concepts to Middle American art, see Kubler (1967: 7).

[13] According to Nicholson (1971: 98), The Palace of the Quetzal Butterfly dates to Late Tlamimilolpan and Early and Late Xolalpan times, ca. A.D. 300–650; C. Millon (1972: 15) places this particular painting in Period 6, the last of her stages for this site. The Palace of the Sun is believed to date to the last epoch before the fall of Teotihuacan (INAH 1966: 40). C. Millon (1972: 15) also assigns this to Period 6. Step-frets are present also at Tetitla in Room 1, Mural 4, and Room 11, Mural 1, a location with foreign (Maya and Zapotec) elements (Miller 1973: 123, Figs. 238, 239; 137, Fig. 279; 150, Fig. 316). According to C. Millon 1972: 12), the long-nosed form associated with the Maya area is also present here.

pak, a sequence of painted step-frets ornaments the risers of a bench-like platform in Room 1, Structure 1, in a manner reminiscent of the decorative step-frets at the Palace of the Quetzal Butterfly, Teotihuacan (compare Figs. 18, 19). Above the platform is a mural depicting a dynastic ceremony focusing on what appears to be the presentation of a royal infant (Kubler 1969: 13).

At the same structure, in the famous battle mural of Room 2, step-frets appear on the clothing of several lavishly dressed men including an unarmed figure in a long red frock who is bending down, possibly tending the wounded (Fig. 20). Perhaps he is a priest of the same family as the noble people in Room 1, and the step-fret functions both as the emblem for a particularly important lineage and as a religious symbol.

Carved Stones

Both religious and dynastic overtones are also suggested for this significant symbol by its context in representations on carved stones from Bonampak and other sites from the Usumacinta River area. Step-frets are found on figures on the tablet of Temple 21, Palenque; Stela 1, Bonampak; and Stela 1 (front), Aguas Calientes (Greene, Rands, and Graham 1972: 18–19, 148–149, 182–183, Pls. 3, 68, 84; Morley 1937–1938: Pl. 50).

In addition, on Lintel 24, Structure 23, Yaxchilán (Fig. 21), step-frets alternating with composite Ts decorate the body of a shallow woven basket. Within the basket lie strips of bark paper spotted with blood and one end of a thorn-studded cord—paraphernalia used for the human blood-letting ritual illustrated on this lintel and elsewhere in Late Classic Maya art (Lintels 15, 17, 25 at Yaxchilán; Stela 2 at Bonampak; Greene, Rands, and Graham 1972: Pls. 33, 35, 36, 69; see also Joralemon 1974).

The event pictured on Lintel 24 centers on two elegantly clad figures. To the right is a kneeling woman engaged in passing the grisly cord through her tongue in an act of autosacrifice. Her clothing is the kind generally worn for ceremonial functions and public occasions: a long dress covered partly by a tunic or *huipil* which resembles a cloak open in the front (Proskouriakoff 1961: 81). Both garments are elaborately decorated with the same overall pattern. This consists of an unbroken latticework frame with straight edges superimposed over a second latticework design with serrated edges, which has within each interior space a double concentric rhomboid infixed with a cross.

Proskouriakoff (1961: 82) has noted that women are particularly important in the art of the Usumacinta area, especially during the Late Classic Period when secular themes and group compositions also attain prominence. More specifically, she (1961: 86–87) states:

The women of Yaxchilan are featured on many sculptured lintels and apparently play here a more important social role than at any other site in the Maya area. In many compositions they share the center of attention equally with men, and their *magnificently embroidered robes are depicted in the finest possible detail* [italics mine].

The attention paid by the sculptor to the minute details of the woman's clothing on Lintel 24 suggests that the design itself may have had special significance for the viewers. An almost identical pattern occurs in Puuc-style stone mosaic form on the exterior walls of the second story of the Epiclassic Monjas (Nunnery) at Chichén Itzá (compare Figs. 4 and 21; see also Charnay 1888: 334). This hints at some kind of formal affiliation between the kneeling lady from Yaxchilán and the elite group responsible for the construction of the upper story of the Monjas, Chichén Itzá. The presence of a sloping profile for the upper façade zone on both the Monjas (a rare trait in structures of this area) and buildings of the Usumacinta, including Yaxchilán, was pointed out before the turn of the century by W. H. Holmes (1895–1897: 109; see also Pollock 1965: 423, 426). This architectural similarity also suggests that there is a linkage between the two sites at the elite level.

The man standing to the left of the woman and holding a decorated wand or torch over her is, according to Proskouriakoff (1963: 153, 156–157,

161), "Shield Jaguar," the greatest of the Yaxchilán rulers, and possibly a foreigner and usurper who gained control of the site through a "military or political coup." As there is no record of formal accession for "Shield Jaguar," Proskouriakoff (1963: 161) proposes that the ruling military group associated with him "was not thoroughly familiar with Classic forms of recording historical dates."

Deeds of "Shield Jaguar," however, are commemorated on both Stelae 18 and 20 at Yaxchilán (Maler 1901, pt. 2: Pls. 77, 78; Proskouriakoff 1963: 160–161), monuments that also bear notations in the Puuc-style of dating which was prevalent in northern Campeche and western Yucatán at that time. This system involves a backward shift of one place in the month positions of the Calendar Round relative to the standard ones found in the southern Maya lowlands (Graham 1973: 207–209; Proskouriakoff and Thompson 1947: 143–150; Thompson 1952: 196–202).

Stelae 18 and 20 at Yaxchilán are also linked stylistically to certain monuments in the Puuc region by the overall style of carving, the pointed shape (of Stela 20), and by particular details such as the rounded outline of the thighs and the short sleeveless jackets worn by the standing figures. This last trait occurs on the carved jambs and the wooden lintel of Structure 1 (Codz Poop) at Kabah in the Puuc area (Proskouriakoff and Thompson 1947: 148; Tozzer 1957: Fig. 603; Stephens 1858, I: opposite 405). In addition, both the standing figure shown on Stela 18, Yaxchilán ("Shield Jaguar"), and that on the carved wooden beam illustrated by Stephens, assume the same body pose, with the torso and legs frontally placed, the feet turned outward, the head in profile, and the left arm slightly bent at the elbow and held at the side.

The scene on Lintel 24, Yaxchilán, has been interpreted in various ways, for example: as "a bloodletting rite expressing the close ritual interaction of male and female dynasts" (Rands in Greene, Rands, and Graham 1972: 84); as "a ceremony of purification after the birth of 'Bird Jaguar,'" successor to "Shield Jaguar" (Proskouriakoff 1963: 164); and, by analogy with the scene on Lintel 17, as an act of "offering to the gods and supernaturals" (Joralemon 1974: 61).

These interpretations are not necessarily in conflict with each other, nor are they complete. It is proposed here that the woman with the distinctive garments is related to nobility in northern Yucatán, most likely from Chichén Itzá, and that this representation symbolizes an alliance made between Yaxchilán and the north through the medium of this important woman. As noted above, women have particular importance during this period (see also Molloy and Rathje 1974). Proskouriakoff (1961: 98) elaborates on this situation:

> Debarred from most public exploits, they [Maya women] have an even greater stake than men in the prestige conferred by a distinguished kinship, and dynastic rivalries are often resolved by the marriage union, which in such circumstances acquires a public importance.

In view of the political value of women noted by Proskouriakoff, and the connections between the monuments of Yaxchilán and northern Yucatán noted above, it seems reasonable to suggest that the kneeling lady on Lintel 24 is demonstrating a new, or perhaps even a continuation of a, political tie with "Shield Jaguar," possibly also the acceptance of a religious faith which involves blood-sacrifice and is symbolized by the step-fret.[14]

Mosaics

Mosaics served as an especially important medium for displaying the step-fret motif. For example, the step-fret appears on either side of a mosaic mask which probably represents a fanged "deity" of the

---

[14] It is my opinion that this faith is associated with a feathered-serpent cult carried into Yucatán by heavily Mexicanized merchants along with fine-orange wares. See Sharp (1975, n.d.b, n.d.c) for elaboration of this thesis. See Bernal, Piña Chan, and Cámara-Barbachano (1968: 124–125, Pl. 90) for an illustration of a "priest" engaged in the blood-letting ritual through tongue sacrifice on a stone monument from Huilocintla, Gulf Coast (Late Classic Period)—evidence of this practice outside the Maya area.

Early Postclassic Period (Fig. 22).[15] This motif is also one of the first that occurs in stone mosaic form as architectural adornment, and it may be present as early as A.D. 400–500 on a substructure at Tajín Chico, Veracruz (García Payón 1971: Table 1). It occurs also at this site during Classic and Epiclassic times as a simple vertical sequence on the Pyramid of the Niches (Fig. 23), and as a simple horizontal band on Structure C, Tajín Chico (Fig. 24). Similar horizontal bands are displayed on the major Pyramid at Lambityeco, Oaxaca (Fig. 25), and on the Iglesia (Church) at Chichén Itzá, Yucatán (Fig. 26), both from the Epiclassic Period.

Such similarities of form and arrangement could have arisen coincidentally. However, a more elaborate pattern, one exhibiting bilateral horizontal symmetry,[16] is found in Oaxaca and Yucatán (Figs. 27, 28), a correspondence that points strongly to inter-regional contact during the Epiclassic Period between these widely separated areas.

Step-fret patterns that display more complex radial biaxial symmetry provide the most impressive evidence for contact for the two regions. For example, the design over the doorway of Tomb 13, Yagul, Oaxaca (Fig. 29), is too close in form, in my opinion, to that appearing on the exterior wall of the Monjas, Chichén Itzá (Fig. 30), to have happened by chance. In each case, the central rhomboid element in these patterns may be a conventionalized substitution for the mask, as it appears in Figure 26, a process which has been described by Spinden (1957: 122–124) in regard to the mask panels in northern Yucatán.

In short, Oaxacans, northern Yucatecans, and people from Veracruz, at least, were participating in a stylistic (and probably ideological) network that was expressed in stone mosaic fretwork decorations on structures for the living and the dead.

[15] This mask is reputed to have been found in the same cave as the Grolier Codex (see fn. 26 below) and a carved wooden box described by Coe (1974: 51–58). It is believed by some authorities to represent "the god Itzamná" (Dumbarton Oaks 1969: no. 449).

[16] The terminology used for the designs described here is that of Shepard (1948: 218, 221).

Pre-Hispanic Meanings

Many people have written about the possible derivations and meanings of the step-fret as it appeared at different times in various Pre-Hispanic Middle American contexts. Without attempting an exhaustive review, I will mention some of these interpretations in order to provide an idea of the range of meanings assigned to this significant visual form.

In a detailed study of the step-fret and related geometric motifs, H. Beyer (1965) advanced the view that the step-fret was principally a formal decorative element, for although he also thought that either serpents or waves could have served as a model for this motif, he did not think that the specific derivation could be determined with the available evidence.

The Nahuatl name used by the Aztecs for this motif was *xicalcoliuhqui*, and the Spanish name was *voluta de jícara* (volute of the gourd; Beyer 1965: 56). In the Codex Magliabechiano (1970: 6r, lower left) representations of blankets bearing step-fret designs are glossed as *manta de xicara tuerta* or "blanket with the crooked gourd [pattern]." Moreover, one early observer, Marshall H. Saville (1920: 160–162), thought that step-frets, when they appeared on shields, were conventionalized representations of the crooked or double gourd traditionally used by native people to carry water. He noted, however, that the design might just as well have been derived from the spiral of a conch shell or from the coil of a snake. Others (Beyer 1965: 56; Caso and Bernal 1952: 161; Westheim 1965: 99; García Payón 1973: 22), in contrast, maintain that the name implies only that this motif was a favorite ornament for potters.

Other scholars have suggested additional, and sometimes multiple, meanings for the motif. For example, Robert Greg (1882: 157–160) thought it represented water, and W. H. Holmes (1895–1897: 53) thought that waves were one possible source of inspiration. Carl Lumholtz (1909: 201) saw a mass of clouds as a possible archetype. Francis Parry (1894: 38) related the step-fret to the wind. José García Payón (1951: 175; 1973: 18) associated the motif at El Tajín with light, sun, and life, and considered it to have been a kind of magical protection against death. Lumholtz (1909: 201) and Saville (1920: 161–162) suggested also that one possible derivation for the step-fret was the serpent, a creature associated with water. Holmes (1895–1897: 250) thought that the mosaic designs, including the step-fret, at Mitla, Oaxaca, were derived from markings on the body of a "serpent deity." Paul Westheim (1965: 102–104) believed that it symbolized lightning or the "Fire Serpent." I think that at one level of meaning, at least during the Epiclassic Period, it represented the "Feathered Serpent" (see fn. 14).

Most, if not all, of these meanings seem plausible. The fact is, they are not mutually exclusive. All pertain to the powers of nature—both its great beneficence and its destructiveness for man. It is probably this multivocality of the symbol that gave it appeal and contributed to its persistence and use in various historical contexts. More specifically, its many possible natural associations, and the implied potency, even deadliness, of this symbol also help to explain why certain elites of Classic and Epiclassic times appear to have chosen it as an emblem, and why it is associated with the T (a symbol for wind and life, at least for the Maya), and with particular masks in more than one Pre-Hispanic Middle American culture.[17]

Oaxacan Masks

The large stone mosaic masks found in the Puuc area and at Chichén Itzá during the Epiclassic and Early Postclassic Periods are one of the most distinctive architectural features of northern Yucatán. This kind of mask is absent, however, from Veracruz and Oaxaca and rare in the southern Maya lowlands,[18] although sculptured masks or long-nosed heads of similar forms do occur both in Oaxaca and in the Maya area in general.

The best-known sculptured product of the Classic Monte Albán (Zapotec) people in Oaxaca is a particular kind of pottery urn which is roughly cylindrical and decorated with a figure on the front (Fig. 8) (Paddock 1966: 128–140). Such figures were assembled from modeled and moulded elements, and were, like the mosaic components of the masks of Yucatán, standardized and interchangeable.[19]

Some time ago Herbert Spinden (1957: 329) called attention to another possible association between Oaxacan urns and Yucatecan masks. He observed that, "Figures similar to those modeled in bold relief on the fronts of the cylindrical funeral urns . . . seem to have been used over doorways [at Oaxacan sites], somewhat after the fashion of the Mayan mask panels." He also believed that these representations were related to the Maya "Long-nosed God" discussed below. Examples are difficult to find now, but Rickards (1910: 132) illustrates one such mask, which is similar to those found in Yucatán, but which displays neither the detail nor the naturalism of many of the urns.

Scholars (Caso and Bernal 1952: 17–49; Paddock 1966: 128, 139) have tended to stress the *divine* nature of the beings represented on the urns, but at least some of these figures appear to me to be idealized portraits (e.g., Caso and Bernal 1952: Figs. 341, 345, 346), a distinction made earlier by Spinden (1957: 329) when he noted that the urns represented both "human beings" and "grotesque divinities" or "human beings wearing the masks of divinities."[20]

Most often represented is Cocijo (Fig. 8), who is referred to by major authorities (Caso and Bernal 1952: 17; Paddock 1966: 135, Fig. 116; Seler 1904:

---

[17] See Munn (1973: 211–221) and Turner (1968: 21) for a discussion of multiple meanings, patterning, and messages.

[18] Mosaic masks are characteristic of the Chenes–Río Bec–Puuc stylistic area in general. Temple 22 at Copán has double tiers of Chac masks of Puuc or Chenes style at each corner. For a discussion of possible relationships between the Puuc area and Copán, see Parsons (1969: 165).

[19] Teotihuacan braziers are also decorated with mold-made, standardized, interchangeable parts. They are conceptually related to, and may be prototypes for, both the Oaxacan urns and mosaic stone sculpture (see Sharp 1978).

[20] See also Spinden (1916: 438–439; Pl. IV). Artists may also have drawn on the features of actual people in modeling the faces of deities, a procedure suggested by Coe (1975: 24) in regard to the figurines from Jaina Island off of the west coast of Yucatán.

300–301) as the "god" of water, rain, and lightning, although he is also very closely associated with the "god" of maize, and wears a similar mask and, at times, the headdress of this "god" (Caso and Bernal 1952: 18–19, Fig. 5).

The mask, which covers all of Cocijo's face, is his most distinctive and constant feature. The eyebrows are crenelated; the lower lids are indented and squared off; volutes extend downwards from the nose and encircle the mouth; a bifurcated tongue projects downward from the open jaws; often, in addition, circular plugs with circular insets adorn the ears (Fig. 8) (Caso and Bernal 1952: 18–19).

Because of his rain and fertility associations, Cocijo is believed to correspond to the Central Mexican "Tlaloc," the Totonac "Tajín," and the Maya "Chac" (Caso and Bernal 1952: 17; Seler 1904: 267). However, the concept of "Cocijo" involves much more than rain and fertility. According to Eduard Seler (1904: 267–271), Cocijo was also associated with a 260-day ritual calendar: "Cocijo" was the name for the four signs, and the first day of the four thirteen-day periods of which this calendar was composed; each of these periods was assigned a compass direction, and the prognostication for each period of time depended on the calendrical and directional position of this all-powerful figure.

In addition, Cocijo has political overtones. In Zapotec, "Cocijo" means "great one" and "the god," and it was also a royal title for Zapotec kings. For example, the king of Tehuantepec at one time was "Cocijo-pij," and another, from a nearby area, was "Cocijo-eza" (Seler 1904: 239, 301).

Representations of supernaturals and individual humans occur in larger sculptural form at Lambityeco in the Valley of Oaxaca. The elaborate Cocijo faces, which are very similar to those on the Cocijo urns (compare Figs. 8 and 9), have been mentioned earlier. In addition, plaster reliefs of a man and a woman were prominently placed over the entry to a nearby tomb (Fig. 31). This naturalistic rendering of specific human beings led one scholar (Rabin 1970: 12) to postulate the presence of a new "secular elite" at this site. Perhaps, however, something somewhat different is being manifested here. Ideal human types, possibly portraits, were present, in my opinion, on the urns. It is the individualized unmasked face and the boldness of the representation that are striking.

Lambityeco is a transitional site, and, like other Epiclassic centers, it reflects both the breaking up of older patterns and the formulation of new ones.[21] The fact that human beings are never again depicted so individually or openly in the Valley of Oaxaca before the Spanish Conquest suggests to me that these portraits represent a culmination of an earlier theocratic value system, rather than a budding secularism. Paradoxically, these faces may have expressed deification, rather than asserted human individualism. The people depicted may have been rulers who had finally equated themselves with the gods during their lifetimes, rather than more mundane aristocrats who had relegated religion to a secondary position.

Had such portraiture been a significant manifestation of a new secular ethos, one would expect to see it perpetuated during the following era (Monte Albán V). Instead, at Mitla (Fig. 32), we see only the continuity and florescence of the kind of repetitious geometric forms present on the Lambityeco pyramid (Fig. 25). Of the buildings they decorate, W. H. Holmes (1895–1897: 245) was to say:

Sculpture in its more restricted and commonly accepted sense seems to have been tabooed as completely as if a priestly edict had been promulgated forever prohibiting it.

Long-nosed Masks in Northern Yucatán

The mosaic stone masks at Chichén Itzá, Uxmal, and the Puuc Hill sites are not all the same—between sites, within sites, and even on the same

---

[21] Paddock (n.d.) states that, at Lambityeco, objects from Monte Albán III, IV, and V appear together. See Proskouriakoff (1955), Sabloff and Rathje (1975), and Sabloff (1977: 91–93) for a parallel discussion of decadence and reformulation at Mayapán, Yucatán.

structures; but there exist both certain basic features that are common to all of the masks and great standardization and interchangeability of parts between individual masks. In addition, old masks were often repaired at later dates with little concern for an exact match with original pieces.[22]

The "ideal" mask (Figs. 15, 26, 33) has: a curled nose (possibly an upper lip in some cases)[23] with a wide variety of profile shapes, a superior nose ornament consisting of a roll-shaped body or a small human face, sometimes nose plugs,[24] either reduced lips or a greatly elongated upper lip, a lateral mouth ornament like a curled fang, a round or rectangular eye (the latter resembling the Cocijo eye), upper and lower teeth, usually square earplugs, a tripartite ear ornament in the form of two frets turned in opposite directions and separated by a horizontal bar, and a headband of beaded discs.[25] As noted earlier, these masks are commonly clustered with T-sequences and step-frets (Figs. 6, 13, 15, 33).

These masks, in general, most closely resemble the long-nosed "Chacs" of the Maya Postclassic manuscripts or codices (folding fig-bark books), which are believed to have been written in Yucatán.[26] They are pictured in these sources engaged in a variety of activities and antics, for example, standing or strolling in the rain, beating a drum, paddling a canoe, arising from a serpent's mouth, brandishing burning torches, riding a deer, urinating, and copulating (Figs. 34, 35). For the contemporary observer, there is a comic-book character about their portrayal, but, very probably, to the native viewer, their business was deadly serious.

In Yucatec Maya iconography, the Chacs were fundamentally "rain gods" and (according to Bishop Landa) "gods" of the cornfields and grains. Like the Oaxacan Cocijos, each of the four principal Chacs was associated with a world direction, a calendrical position, and a color—East–red, North–white, West–black, South–yellow (Fig. 34) (Thompson 1970a: 251–253).[27]

Since the time of the first identification and delineation of supernatural figures in the codices by Paul Schellhas (1884, German; 1904, English), Chacs have generally been identified with "God B" of his classification system (Schellhas 1904: 16–19; Spinden 1957: 62–69). Although details vary slightly among the codices, representations of God B have human bodies and grotesque heads, which may be masks (Fewkes 1894: 232, 266, 269). These are characterized by a long pendulous nose, a scroll behind the eye, a curved projection above the mouth, and, frequently, a similar fang-like object dangling from the center of the upper jaw (Fig. 35, top figure).[28]

Figural representations of God B in the codices are often accompanied by a particular glyph (T–668; Thompson 1962: 264–265), the basic form of which represents the back of a clenched fist, with a "jade bead" at the wrist (Fig. 36c). The fist is personified by a vestigial nose and mouth and a T-shaped symbol for an eye. A second glyph (T–103; Thompson 1962: 50) is usually affixed to the principal one. In

[22] Tozzer (1957: 34) notes that the third story of the Monjas (Nunnery), Chichén Itzá, was constructed of re-used stones. The Iglesia (Church) also shows evidence of having been rebuilt in later times: particular mouth ornaments on the central mask do not match; other elements of the mask appear to have been made over from stones taken from another place.

[23] For a discussion of "long-nosed" vs. "long-lipped" deities, see Joralemon (1974: 63).

[24] These are present today at the Palomas group, Uxmal, and they were probably present on the Iglesia and the Temple of the Warriors, Chichén Itzá (see Morris, Charlot, and Morris 1931, I: 27).

[25] Spinden (1957: 121–122) provides traits for the "ideal" mask. This is a modification of his statement in the light of more recent findings.

[26] Thompson (1975: 1–9) accepts only the Dresden, Madrid, and Paris, but not the Grolier Codex, as genuine. See Coe (1973: 150–154) for the opposite viewpoint. As evidence that the Maya Postclassic manuscripts were written in Yucatán, Thompson (1970a: 257) cites the fact that the Chac glyph (T–668) in the manuscripts occurs only at Chichén Itzá and Uxmal, and not elsewhere.

[27] This quadripartite concept was not limited to the Chacs. There are at least two other supernatural clusters—the Pahuatuns and the Bacabs—that have directional qualities and are associated with rain, wind, and fertility. Chacs, Pahuatuns, and Bacabs merge in many places, and the precise relationships among the three are not clear. For a detailed discussion of these concepts, see Thompson (1934; 1970a: 276–280; 1970b), Tozzer (1941: 135–136, fn. 632; 137, fn. 638); also Coe (1975: 25).

[28] This is a modification of Thompson's (1970a: 252) description.

the Dresden Codex, the glyph may also be personified (Fig. 36b) (Dresden 32c, 36b, 38b), in which
case it resembles more closely the face or mask of
the figural representations (Fig. 36a).

Long-nosed masks believed to represent God B
or Chacs are also found in painted reliefs at Chichén
Itzá. For example, at the Temple of the Warriors on
the dais of the northwest colonnade, south side, the
first two figures in a procession wear hat-masks and
face-masks, both having long noses. Similar figures
are found on the north side of this dais, and also at
the Temple of the Chac Mool (Figs. 37, 38) (Morris,
Charlot, and Morris 1931, I: 237–238, 367–381; II:
Pls. 33–34, 127, 129, 133).

The elongated and curved nose, the lateral pro-
jections at the sides of the mouth, and the noseplugs
found on the figures in these reliefs and on the
personification glyph of God B in the Dresden Codex are very similar to those on the mosaic masks.
The relief representations that are most similar to
the stone masks are those on the base and capitals of
the sculptured pilasters at the Temple of the Chac
Mool (compare Figs. 26, 33, and 39).

Various authorities have confidently identified
and isolated God B from other figures in the codices
and other media, but the conceptual boundaries
between the so-called "gods" during the Postclassic, and probably even more so during the Epiclassic, Period were relatively fluid. To be more
specific, in the codices, Chacs (God B) have an
especially close association with God K, a figure
who also had a long, but more elaborate (or "foliated"), up-turned nose. A not uncommon representation is that of a Chac in close association with,
or emerging from (or being swallowed by), a serpentine form bearing a head identified by Günter
Zimmermann (1956: 165–166) as that of God K
(Fig. 35) (Dresden 33b, 34b, 35b; Madrid 31b).
Chacs also wear head-masks of God K (Dresden
34b, 65a; Zimmermann 1956: 166; Schellhas 1904:
32). In fact, the intimate relationship between these
two deities led some early observers to consider
God B as simply a manifestation of God K (Spinden
1957: 64).[29]

God B, however, is also related to God D. In the
Dresden Codex (34c, 41a), he is shown seated on a
cauac element with the head of God D at one end
(Thompson 1972: 97, 104; see also Spinden 1957:
75, Fig. 97a, b; and Coe 1973: 98, 107 for discussions of the Cauac Monster). He is also associated
with the Moon Goddess and the Red Goddess of
Weaving (Dresden 38a, 42b; Thompson 1972: 96,
101), for whom he seems to have more than a
passing fancy. In addition, according to Spinden
(1957: 62), some authorities have associated God B
with Itzam Na, whom Thompson (1973a: 54, 58)
considers to be the supreme god of the Classic Maya,
the giver of rain, and the greatest of the Yucatec
gods as well. Finally, others have considered God B
to represent Kukulcán (or Quetzalcoatl), the Feathered Serpent (see Spinden 1957: 62).

Therefore, in attempting to relate Postclassic pictorial representations of God B to the mosaic stone
masks of the Epiclassic and Early Postclassic Periods, this cosmological confusion should be kept in
mind. Although some dissimilarities between masks
can at times be explained on the basis of differences
in space and time, others may be related to the
fluidity of the concepts that are involved. There is
no reason to assume that the same cluster of concepts is being represented in each mask, that any one
representation bears attributes of only one "deity,"
or that the same value was being placed on any
particular concept through time.

I do believe, however, that the vast majority of
the masks at Chichén Itzá, and probably at other
northern Yucatecan sites, represent primarily the
cluster of traits attributed to the Chacs. Both the
basic similarity of elements of the mosaic masks and
the lack of concern for an exact match in restoring
old ones at later dates suggest that as time went on
the general concept manifested in the total product
was more important than the exact details of the
mask itself.

---

[29] Some of the stone mosaic masks have long noses or snouts
which turn upward in the manner of Schellhas's God K, e.g.,
those on the exterior of the Pyramid of the Magicians (Fig. 42)
and on the East Building of the Monjas, Uxmal; but the nose is
not "foliated" in these instances as it is in the codex representations. (See also Foncerrada de Molina 1965: Figs. 2, 18.)

Maya Masks and Monarchs

Both the form and construction of the Yucatecan stone mosaic masks remind one of the Cocijo faces of the Oaxacan urns and Lambityeco sculptured pieces. In both places, masks, T-sequences, and step-frets are additionally found in close association in an iconographic cluster that involves natural forces and focuses on a long-nosed "rain deity." These analogies suggest that other parallel factors may be present as well. Determining specific relationships, however, among ideological, political, and artistic systems is an especially complex problem in this setting.

To begin with, there is disagreement among authorities concerning the religious system itself. Can one identify and delineate specific "gods" among the many images of Maya art, and if so, how do these relate to rulers?

On the one hand, George Kubler (1969: 35) maintains:

> It is difficult to find gods in Classic Maya art. The rulers and priests wear emblems and carry signs, but they rarely if ever submit to godly authority.

According to Kubler (1969: 41, 42, 46), long-nosed masks worn by ruler figures were neither gods nor heads of gods. Their long-nosed helmets functioned as badges; and later long-nosed badges, along with other badges, possibly signified lineages, duties or honors, or had several meanings.

In contrast, other scholars working in this area maintain that the long-nosed representations in the Classic Period were gods, and that rulers became gods themselves during their lifetimes. J. Eric Thompson, a leading exponent of this view, says (1973a: 58, 65) that the Maya rulers had every reason to lay claim to divine rights, and that they very probably associated themselves with Itzam Na, the greatest of their gods. Itzam Na, according to Thompson, appears in several aspects, one of which is God K, who symbolizes (for Thompson) the terrestrial and vegetal domain of life. He notes that

chief rulers are commonly costumed in headdresses that include the deity, or they hold a ceremonial bar (a miniature two-headed Itzam) as on Lintel 1, Lacanhá, or a manikin scepter (a staff terminating in the head of God K) as on Lintel 42, Structure 42, Yaxchilán.

In support of this position, Linda Schele (1976: 15) maintains that the rulers of Palenque, Chiapas, were considered living divinities, and she identifies in the Palencano art specific instances of deification of two rulers, Chan-Bahlum and Pacal. According to Schele, these rulers were not simply people wearing the attributes of gods; they were living incarnations of God K.[30]

At Palenque, specific rulers and their families are identifiable by regular physical features, and perhaps even by genetic anomalies.[31] Moreover, probably nowhere in Pre-Hispanic Middle American art is portraiture more highly developed than at this site (Fig. 40). It seems reasonable that men declared divine in their lifetimes need not have hidden behind masks to assert their divinity.

Whether we see long-nosed heads or masks in Classic Maya art as nature spirits or coded deities, by the end of this period such supernaturals seem to have suffered a kind of devaluation in the hands of men. They are neither separate from, nor greater than, particular human beings. Either they are emblems that assert the religious, social, and political status of high chiefs and their families, or they are badges of divine legitimacy for individual monarchs. If, as Thompson suggests and Schele asserts, rulers at southern Maya lowland centers became

---

[30] Rulers appear to be asserting divinity during their lifetimes on the sarcophagus lid in the Tomb of the Inscriptions, and on the piers of the Temple of the Inscriptions, Palenque (Schele 1976: 15), and on Zoomorph P, Quiriguá (Thompson 1973a: 69, Fig. 10).

[31] See Schele (1974: 49, Fig. 9). Greene Robertson, Scandizzo, and Scandizzo (1976) have isolated what they believe are particular genetic traits in nobles at Palenque.

divine in their lifetimes, a last-ditch kind of leash on rulers by the ruled had been lost.

But perhaps this was not to last. As Thompson (1973a: 69) comments:

Assumption of such divine rank may well have bolstered their control of their principalities until, at last, the underlings raked in their graves and proved them men.

The Chacs: A Cosmological Model

As individual Classic civilizations in their respective areas were failing, new ways of life associated with the inter-regional phenomenon termed "Epiclassic" were being formulated. As was stated earlier, this transition involved the redefining, redesigning, and reassigning of power.

One model for these changes available to leaders in northern Yucatán was the Chac concept. Chacs were intimately associated with the most potent natural forces and, because of the fluidity of the cosmological system, with the most powerful of elites as well. But the concept also contained an internal mechanism for the limitation of power.

In my opinion, the most crucial feature of the Chac concept was the quadripartite and rotational nature of the Chacs themselves. The four principal Chacs moved in order throughout an era in such a way that the impact and power of each was divided, and the promise was always present that no matter how terrible some times were, good days would come.

An especially good illustration of this cosmological system as it is expressed in visual arts is present on pages 42c–45c of the Dresden Codex (Fig. 34), (Thompson 1972; Codex Dresden 1930: 94–100), the probable meanings of which are provided by Thompson (1972: 106–197). On Dresden 42c, "A Chac . . . menaces with upraised axe a seated figure . . . the maize god." The prophecy is "drought . . . woe to the maize god." In contrast, on Dresden 43c, "A Chac paddles a canoe." To one side are offerings of an iguana and maize. The prophecy is one of "very good tidings . . . abundance of maize." The third Chac in this sequence, on Dresden 44c, is pictured with Zimmermann's God W, possibly a masked Chac. They seem to be making divine offerings. The prophecy is "abundance of maize." The final picture, Dresden 45c, shows God B holding torches and sitting astride a dying deer with its head twisted upward and its tongue hanging out to denote thirst. The prophecy is "evil for the maize god . . . drought . . . death." The overall interpretation by Thompson is: "The Chacs at the four world directions are offered food. In two [instances] good crops are promised; in two, drought and death are man's lot" (Thompson 1972: 106).

In short, like Oaxacan Cocijos, Chacs imply a great deal more than rain. The Chac concept provided both an explanatory device for, and a systematic way of, ordering the good and bad events that befall man, especially in his dominant role as maize farmer. Belief in the symbolic system gave even the least powerful person a feeling of having some control over nature and his or her own life.

Stone mosaic Chacs, and the Ts and step-frets with which they were associated, made up a complex of old and very powerful images. Such Chacs can be viewed as repetitious visual chants involving nature's ups and downs, spelled out more exactly in the codices, and in the rituals represented in the carved and painted reliefs noted above for Chichén Itzá (Fig. 37). But they also may be seen as a visual manifestation of a new political system in northern Yucatán.

The Chiefs

Any attempt to characterize the chiefs, and to determine the precise nature of political organization for the Epiclassic Period in northern Yucatán, without contemporary historical records, complete archaeological evidence from carefully controlled excavations, or even a generally accepted chronological sequence for that time period, is admittedly limited. It must rest primarily upon documents written during the Colonial Period (but referring to earlier times), on iconographic analysis, and on ethnographic analogies.

For our purposes, the writings of Bishop Diego de Landa from about 1566 (Tozzer 1941), *The Chilam Balam of Chumayel* (Roys 1967), and the *Ritual of the Bacabs* (Roys 1965) provide the best documentary sources. The first of these represents a detailed description of Yucatec Maya life and culture at the time of the Conquest. The Chilam Balam books and possibly much of the *Ritual of the Bacabs*, according to Thompson (1972: 12), were probably derived from earlier "authorized texts" for oral versions of prophecies, recitations, and songs.

For visual study, we have geometric motifs, relatively rare examples of naturalistic forms, such as huts, serpents, and soldiers, and a few representations of particular people carved in stone and wood at some of the Puuc sites and at Chichén Itzá. The traits exhibited in these latter representations suggest that we are dealing with a mixture of native Maya and foreign peoples, although the precise nature of the latter is not completely understood.[32]

In addition, Michael D. Coe (1965) has provided a particularly thoughtful and provocative ethnohistorical model that relates cosmological and political systems in this area. In this, Coe speculated about the possible forms of Maya social and political organization at the community level, using the Uayeb or New Year's Rites described by Landa as a model. He found evidence for "some sort of quadripartite division of the ancient Maya community, arranged according to cardinal directions and with color associations; for the shifting of ritual power among these divisions in a counterclockwise fashion through a cycle of four years; and for the holding of power by a different *principal* [official] each year" (Coe 1965: 103).

Coe also noted that these New Year's rites may have provided a model that could have been replicated on higher levels than that of the community: Chichén Itzá, for example, according to the *Second Chronicle of Chumayel*, during Katun 4 Ahau (a Maya time period) was made up of four quarters associated with four world directions; Mayapán, a city of a later period, according to the *Third Chronicle of Chumayel*, also had four divisions. He (1965: 109–110) suggested further that calendrical permutations may have been used as an automatic device to rotate power among equal segments at the state level, just as they seem to have been at the community level.

Coe's model of Pre-Conquest government in Yucatán and the cosmological model of the Chacs described earlier are mutually reinforcing, and both are buttressed by additional data from documentary sources.

As proposed above, the essential features of the Chacs were their quadripartite nature, involving a combination of conceptual oppositions of good and bad, and their rotation through time. Chacs were, moreover, related to historical chiefs. According to one *Chronicle of Chumayel*, *The Rise of Hunac Ceel to Power*, and Ralph Roys's (1967: 66–76) interpretation of it, before the Spanish Conquest in Yucatán, "Chac" was an important political title, just as "Cocijo" apparently was in Oaxaca. One of the first rulers at Uxmal was called Hun-Uitzil-Chac, and the title apparently was retained by subsequent rulers (Roys 1967: 66, fn. 9; 67, fn. 5). "*Chac . . .* is an

---

[32] For a discussion of the distinctions between Classic Maya and foreign traits at Chichén Itzá, see Proskouriakoff (1970: 457–467), Sharp (1975), Tozzer (1957), and Thompson (1970a).

adjective signifying 'red,' 'great,' or 'severe'" in Yucatec (Thompson 1970a: 252), and would have been an appropriate title for a political leader.

In addition, Roys notes that in the *Chronicle from Mani*, Chac-Xib-Chac is said to be the head-chief of Chichén Itzá. Landa says Chac-Xib-Chac is also one of the names of the Red Bacab, a deity intimately associated with the Red Chac or rain god of the East (see fn. 27). Roys (1967: 67, fn. 5) states:

> Here we have an important personage bearing the name of the rain-god, and we may infer that he figured as the representative of the god.

He refers to the ritual illustrated on the South Bench of the Temple of the Chac Mool (Fig. 38), mentioned above, in which four men are pictured wearing the mask of God B. They are dressed in jaguar-skin costumes, and are holding manikin scepters—both symbols of royal power. Portraits of individual man-gods are absent. Here are men, masked to make rule legitimate. Royal power in this northern Yucatecan site is thus reconciled with a symbolic model of authority, which is rotating and limiting.

Moreover, we learn from the *Second Chronicle of Chumayel* that the lords of the people who discovered Chichén Itzá were in four divisions, depending on the direction from which they came. According to Roys (1967: 139), these four divisions represented four different groups of people who became amalgamated into one "nation."[33]

Elaborating on Roys's interpretation, Proskouriakoff(1970: 466) proposes that these people, called the Itzá, were "a military group composed of armies of several states . . . a 'confederation,' rather than a 'nation,'" with an alliance based on military and political unity. She postulates further that they modeled their organization after the pattern of a previous conquest.[34]

Although Proskouriakoff (1970: 466) suggests that this model originated in the Toltec-dominated period at Chichén Itzá, i.e., the Early Postclassic, it may well have existed also during the Epiclassic Period. Interpretations of historical events for these periods are confused and contradictory. At least one source, Alfredo Barrera Vasquez (Barrera Vasquez and Morley 1949: 31, fn. 28), believes that the "Itzás" occupied Chichén Itzá between A.D. 495 and 692, a period that corresponds roughly with the manifestation of stone mosaic sculpture at this site according to radiocarbon dating.[35] Moreover, the exact relationship between Epiclassic people and Early Postclassic Toltec-Maya at this site is far from clear, since the two manifestations overlap. There is, in fact, one structure, Casa Colorada, on which there is a "Toltec-Maya"–style relief of marching warriors *beneath* a Puuc-style structure (Fig. 41), an inversion of the expected order.[36]

Also, we know from the *Ritual of the Bacabs* (primarily a book of medical incantations or spells) that in Yucatec society every person at birth was ascribed a fauna (e.g., bird) and a tree, with implied colors and directions. Closely associated with the tree was the "arbor" or "small hut" that the "first men" of certain lineages were assigned in a particular ritual (Roys 1965: xiv, xxii, 63–74). This system for the organization of ritual may have provided a model for maintaining separate groups within the larger

[33] Roys (1967: 139; 139, fn. 5) suggests that the division of the Maya nation into four parts may have been a Nahua (highland Central Mexican) innovation. Coe (1965: 109) thinks that the idea of a city divided into quarters is an idea shared by Central Mexicans and the Maya.

[34] Barrera Vasquez believes that the Itzá were Maya of the "Old Empire," i.e., the southern Classic Maya area (1949: 24, 31, fn. 28; 33, fn. 33–35); Morley believes they were "Mexican" or at least that the leadership was Mexican (Barrera Vasquez and Morley 1949: 71); Thompson (1970a: 3–4, 10–25) sees the Itzá as a branch of the seafaring Putun Maya. See also Kelley (1968: 260).

[35] Radiocarbon dates for buildings at Chichén Itzá having stone mosaic sculpture are as follows: Iglesia— 600±70, 780±70; Casa Colorada—610±70; Monjas—East Patio (?), 810±200 (Andrews IV 1975: 63, Table 5); see also Andrews V (1979: 4, Table 1).

[36] For a discussion of cultural sequences at Chichén Itzá, see Parsons (1969: 172–185).

society. These groups, in turn, may at one time have represented the component parts of an Itzá confederation, such as that postulated by Proskouriakoff. If so, the small huts found within the stone mosaic work at Uxmal and Labná might represent the small huts of the separate groups (Fig. 5).[37] Further research must follow intuition here, however.

Finally, in the *Rise of Hunac Ceel to Power* in the *Chilam Balam of Chumayel* it is stated (Roys 1967: 76):

Katun 8 Ahau came. 8 Ahau was the name of the katun when their government occurred. Then there was a change of the katun, then there was a change of rulers.

I think this hints at a kind of rotational system of rulers at the *state* level in Pre-Conquest times in northern Yucatán, and at a period of office for a particular group of one Katun, or slightly less than twenty years (7200 days).

Transitions and Transformations

It is proposed here that Epiclassic people in northern Yucatán, in a time of transition and crisis, utilized a cosmological model for a political purpose, and that the resulting conflation of sacred and secular systems was manifested in an artistic form which combined particularly potent natural symbols with a quadripartite plan for the limitation of power.

Modern states are not likely to use cosmic models for secular purposes, but pre-modern, pre-industrial societies throughout the world have used "celestial archetypes" both in the laying out of capitals and cities and in the administration of centers and peripheral areas (Wheatley 1971: 411–488; Tambiah 1976: 102–131). Within Middle America, Classic Teotihuacan in particular had a quadripartite city plan which may have reflected both a cosmology involving the four cardinal directions and a four-part social and political organization.[38] In addition, in northern Yucatán, Chichén Itzá, as noted by Coe (1965), was probably at one time made up of four quarters associated with the four world directions. Finally, there is some evidence that cosmic models were being used by Epiclassic and Postclassic peoples not only as a leash on political leaders, but also as paradigms for stable everyday behavior during those rapidly changing times (Sharp n.d.d).

Both the emphasis on old symbols and the attempt to extend control from the natural to the

---

[37] For an alternate, but not necessarily contradictory, interpretation of the iconography of the small huts of the façades of Puuc buildings, see Thompson (1973b: 205–207). For some contrasting interpretations of other Puuc and Chenes–style façades, see Thompson (1939).

[38] Teotihuacan was arranged in a cruciform shape, divided into quadrants by a dominant north-south, and a subordinate east-west axis (R. Millon 1973: 37). Kubler (1967: 8, Fig. 41) has suggested that directions, cults, and the quadrants of Teotihuacan may be symbolized on the Calpulalpan bowl, and that the "goggle-eyed" figure in the center of this bowl may symbolize Teotihuacan as a whole. See also C. Millon (1973) and Becker (1975: 230). Four-part conceptual thinking involving time, space, and cosmology was manifested also in both the Codex Fejérváry-Mayer (1971: 1), a manuscript of the Borgia group, which may have originated in Veracruz (Nicholson 1966: 261; see also Glass and Robertson 1975: 128), and the Codex Madrid (1967: 75–76), from the lowland Maya area (Glass and Robertson 1975: 153; see also fn. 26 above).

18

political realm through use of the Chac concept can be understood best within their historical setting. The collapse of Classic Maya civilization involved invasions, pestilence, and general disruption.[39] These were times when any fundamental human responses that exist are most likely to be evident, and cultural overlays are most likely to be stripped away.

Comparisons between cultures from different times and places should be used with caution. However, a similar situation has been described by Millard Meiss (1973), which might shed some light on the case under discussion. In Florence and Siena in the middle of the fourteenth century, a general state of disorder followed the Black Death and related economic and political crises. This resulted in "more intense piety or religious excitement" (Meiss 1973: 67). Masses of people interpreted the calamities that had befallen them as punishments for their worldliness and sin. Pilgrimages and self-inflicted suffering became especially popular. In addition, guilt and fear of further punishment from God united people in a desire for a more religious art, in contrast to the preceding humanistic form in which the relation of "man to man" was becoming as important as the relation of "man to God" (Meiss 1973: 60, 75–78, 81).

We do not know what Late Classic/Epiclassic Middle Americans thought, or whether or not they suffered the same kind of guilt. We do have evidence for pilgrimages,[40] increased human sacrifice, and the continuation of the ritualistic practice of blood-letting into the Postclassic Period (Joralemon 1974). Moreover, in Late Classic Maya art at Palenque, and possibly in the highland Mexican area as well, at least at the elite level, it appears that the relation of "man to man" had become as important as that of "man to god," and also that the barrier between man and god had broken down altogether. The almost complete absence or clear recessiveness of human representations and portraiture on public structures in northern Yucatán and Oaxaca associated with Epiclassic and Early Postclassic manifestations may well represent a reaction to this situation, analogous to that described by Meiss.

In conclusion, stone mosaic sculpture—with its Ts, step-frets, and masks, provided a new kind of artistic system, one that used old symbols with new inter-regional political implications. Through this art form, a statement could be made concerning both the potency and the limitations of earthly authority. As such, it represented a dynamic compromise involving both a return to a more religious art emphasizing natural forces, and an attempt to develop a symbolic model for the division of power.

We have some evidence that chiefs, like Chacs, did, in fact, rotate their offices in Pre-Conquest times. Bad rulers and bad times could be followed by good rulers and good times—as Chacs who brought drought, famine, and death could be followed by others who brought rain, abundance, and good tidings. In short, the stone mosaic sculptural style of northern Yucatán represented an attempt to restructure a society by providing a powerful symbolic model which could be copied in the real world.

---

[39] For a general discussion of the collapse of Classic Maya civilization, see Culbert (1973); for a discussion of plagues in the Postclassic Period, see Roys (1967: 122; 133, fn. 11), and Thompson (1958: 297–308).

[40] For a discussion of pilgrimages to Puuc sites and to Chichén Itzá, see Brainerd (1958: 29); Thompson (1966: 133–135); Tozzer (1941: 54–56; 109, fn. 500; 139, fn. 648; 140, fn. 652; 180, fn. 947–948).

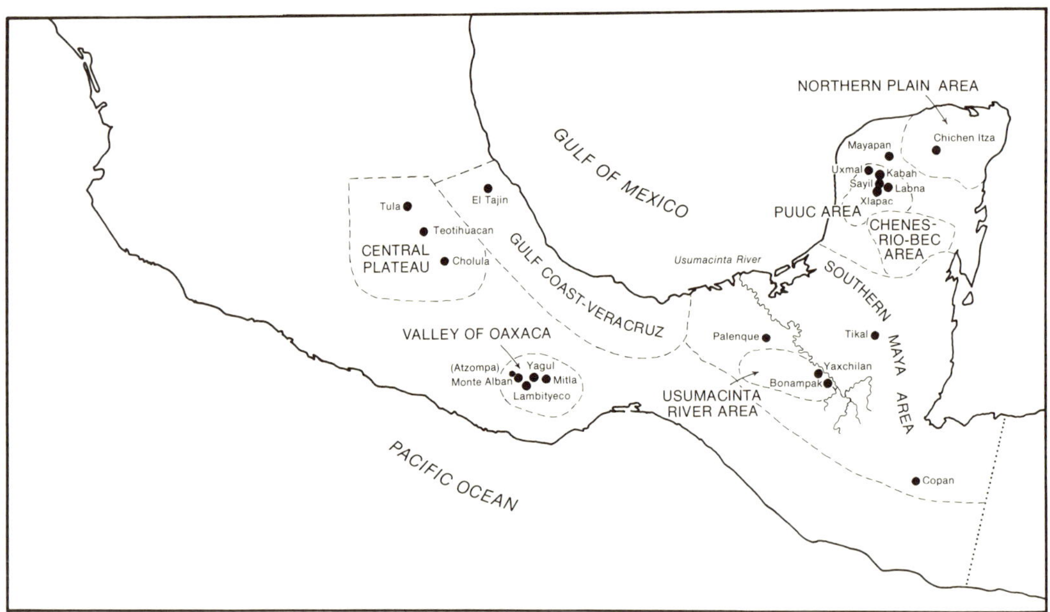

Fig. 1   Map of Pre-Hispanic Mesoamerica showing major archaeological sites mentioned in the text. Drawing by Whitney Powell.

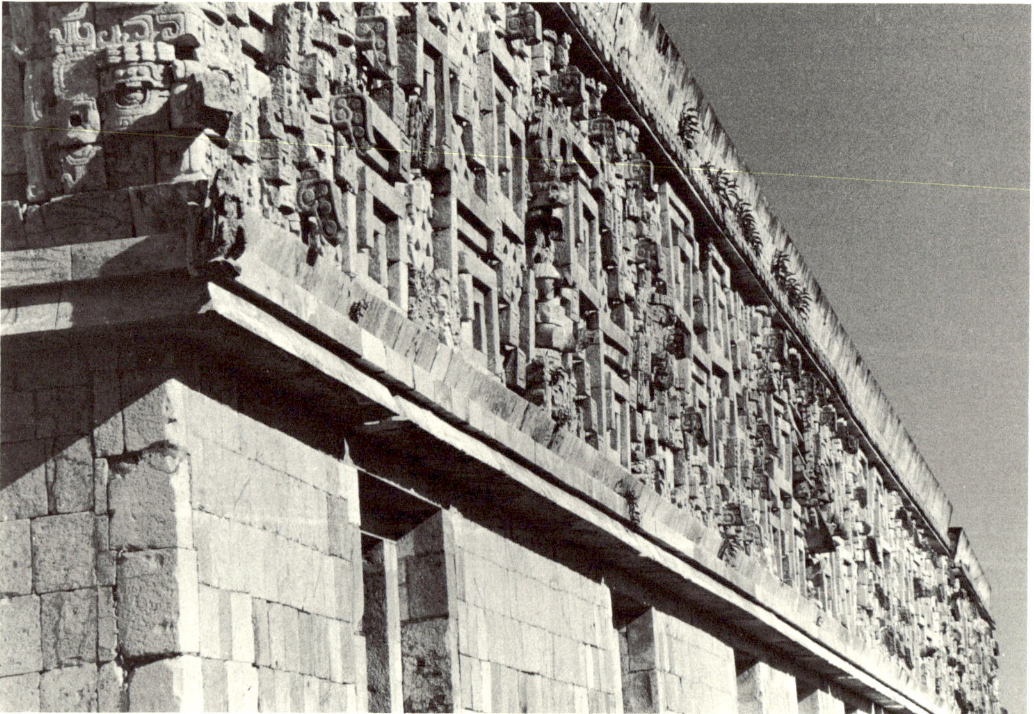

Fig. 2   Mosaic stone sculpture, East Façade, Palace of the Governors, Uxmal, Yucatán. Photo by the author.

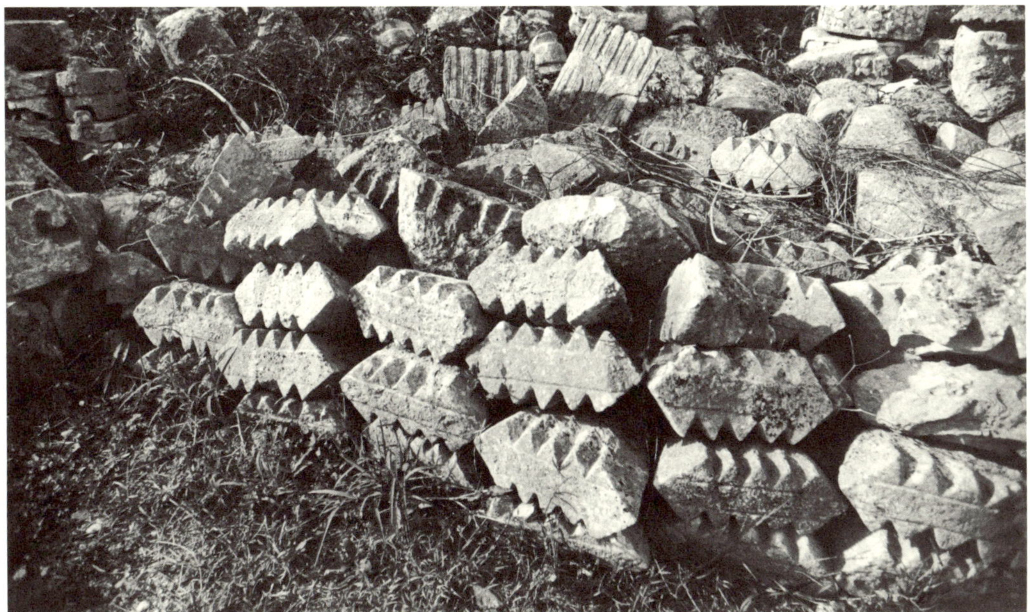

Fig. 3   Pieces of carved stone with serrated edges used in stone mosaic decoration of Puuc–style buildings in northern Yucatán. Photo by the author.

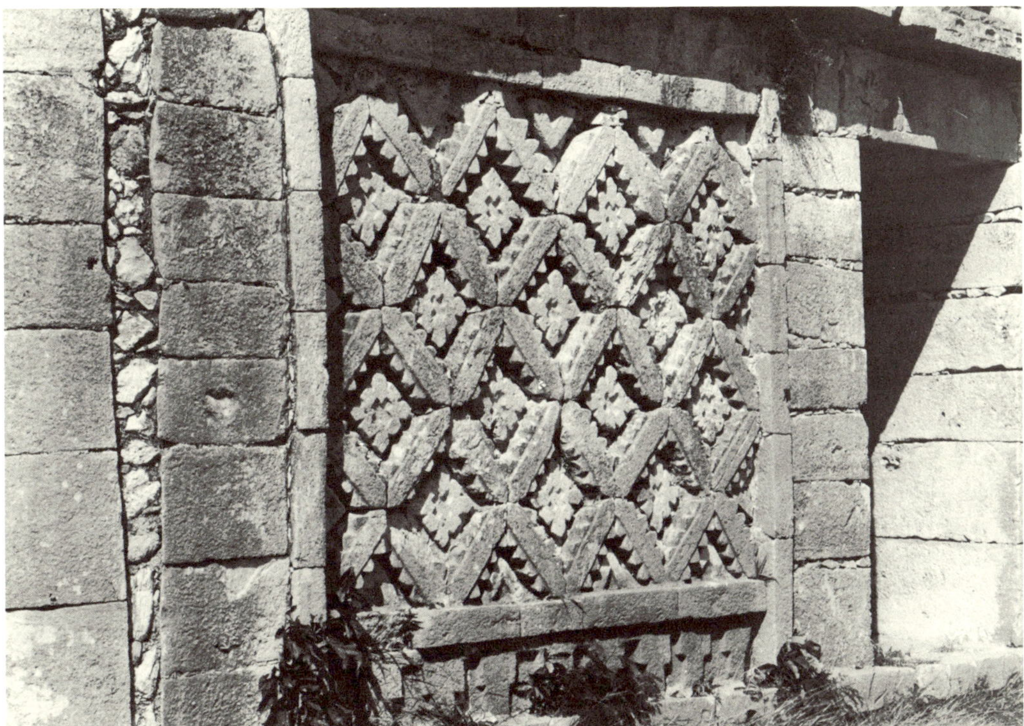

Fig. 4   Mosaic stone sculpture composed of elements with serrated edges, second story, the Monjas (Nunnery), Chichén Itzá, Yucatán. Photo by the author.

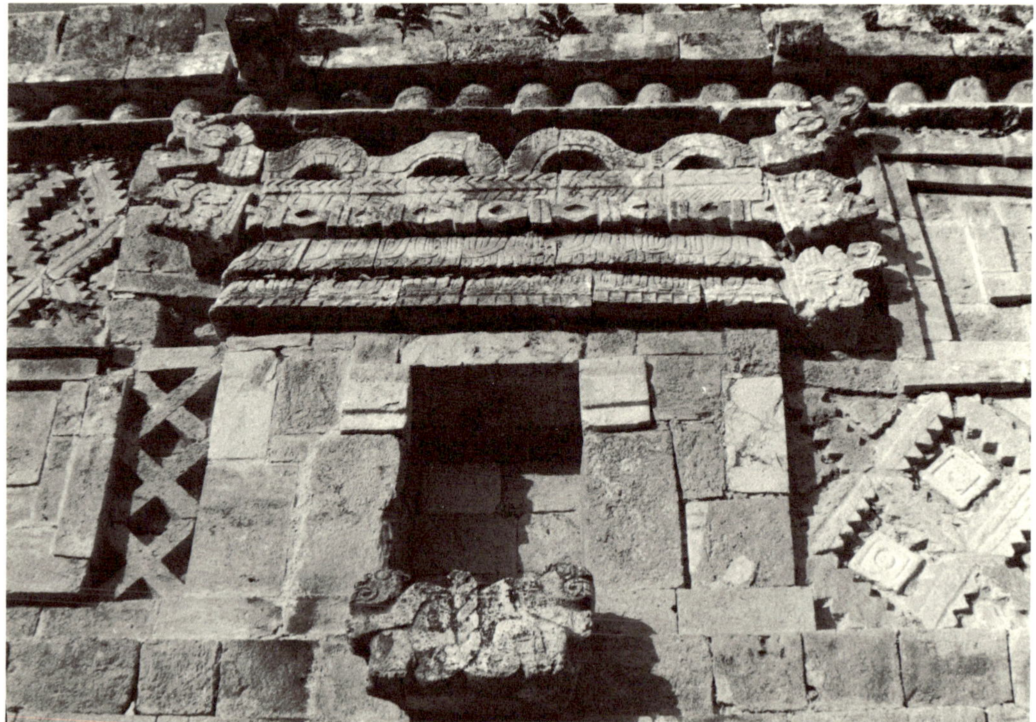

Fig. 5   Detail of small hut, North Building, the Monjas, Uxmal, Yucatán. Photo by the author.

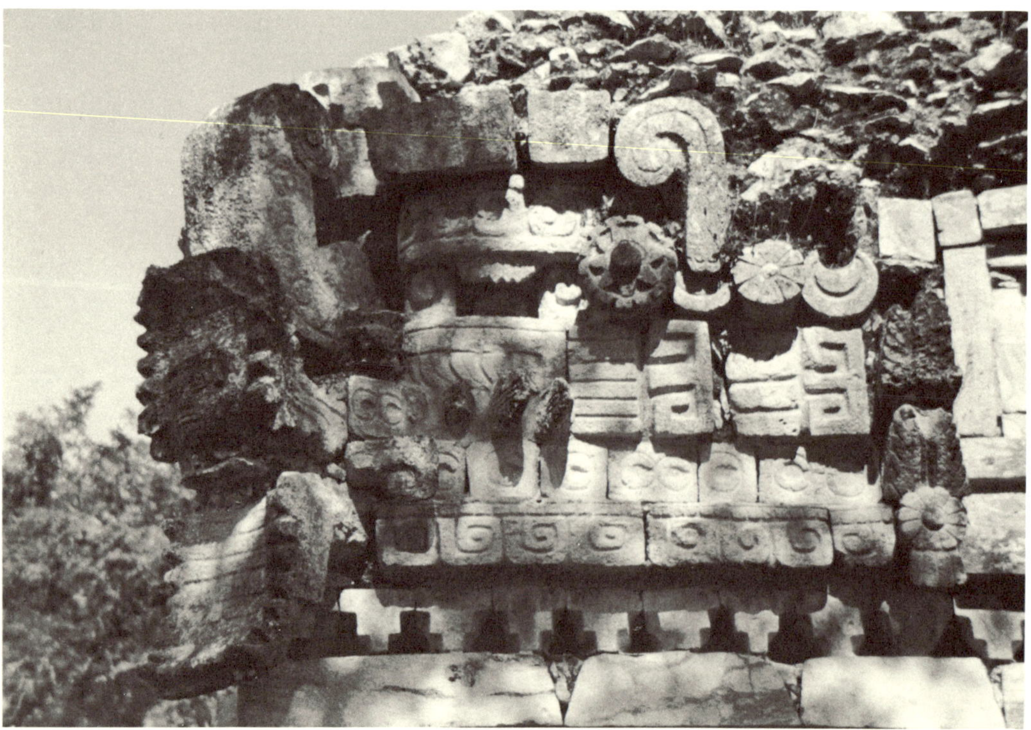

Fig. 6   Sequence of T-forms in association with a mosaic mask, corner of the East Wing, Palace, Labná, Yucatán. Photo by the author.

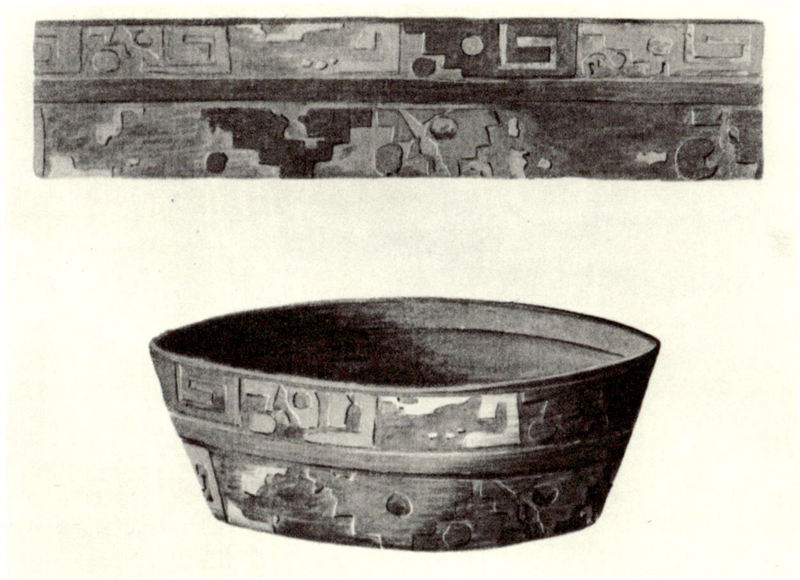

Fig. 7   Monte Albán II pottery from Oaxaca, showing bands of step-pyramids and step-frets (after Caso, Bernal, and Acosta 1967: Lám. IIId).

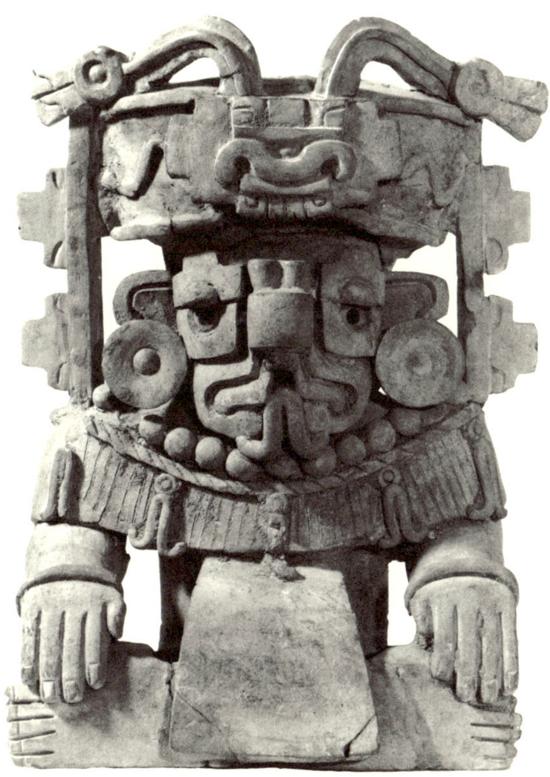

Fig. 8   Classic (Zapotec) urn from Oaxaca showing the "rain god" Cocijo. Photo courtesy of Birmingham Museum of Art, Birmingham, Alabama.

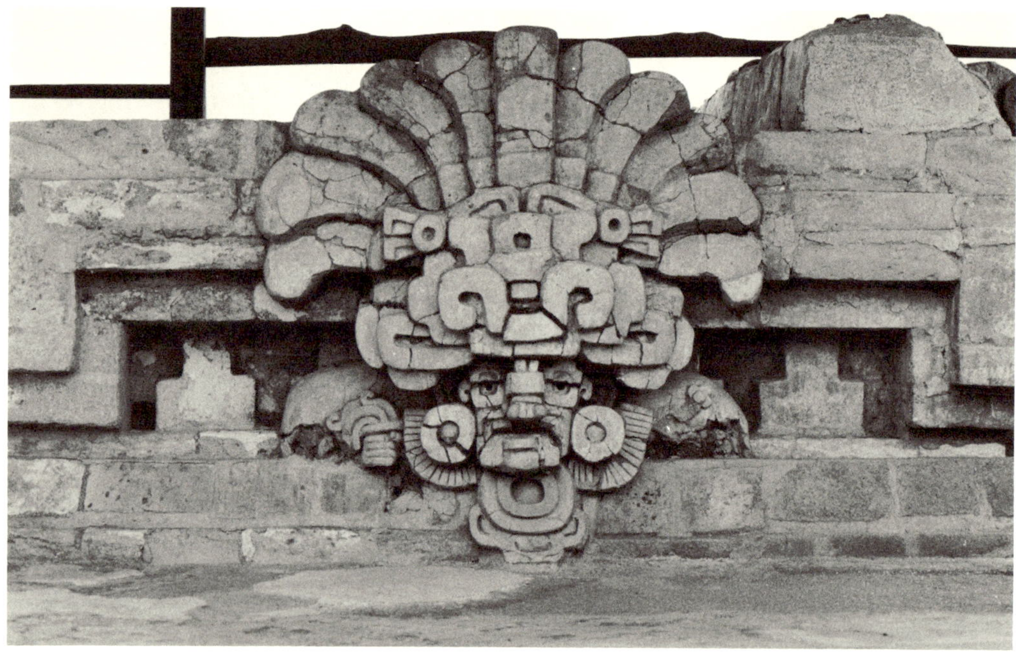

Fig. 9   Cocijo mask in association with sequence of inverted Ts, Lambityeco, Oaxaca (Monte Albán IV). Photo by the author.

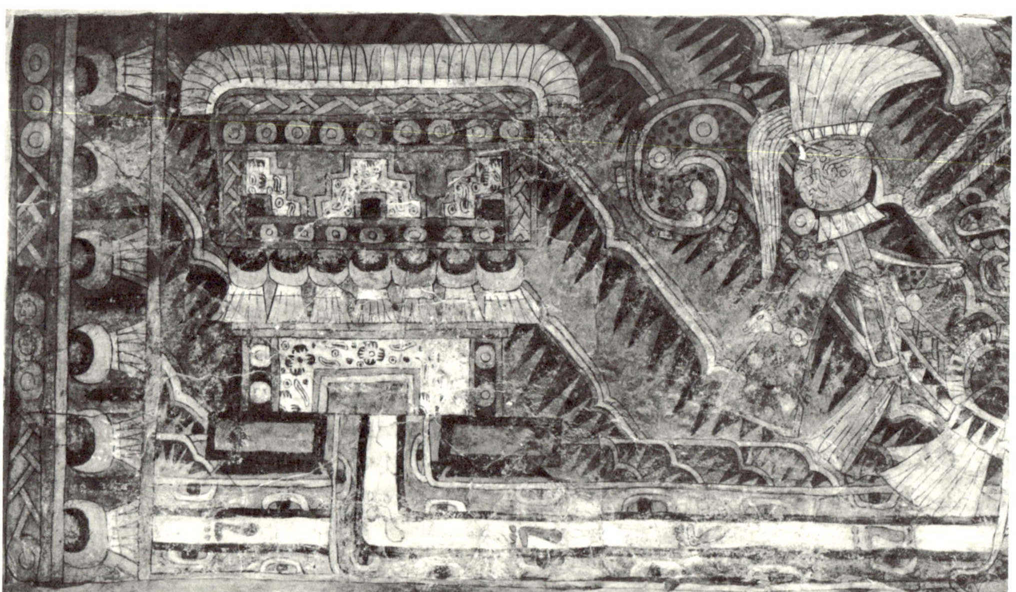

Fig. 10   Step-pyramids used as crenelations on top of a structure in Mural 8, Room 2, Tetitla, Teotihuacan, México. Photo by Nickolas Muray. (Access. No. B-62.TF) Dumbarton Oaks Collections, Washington, D.C.

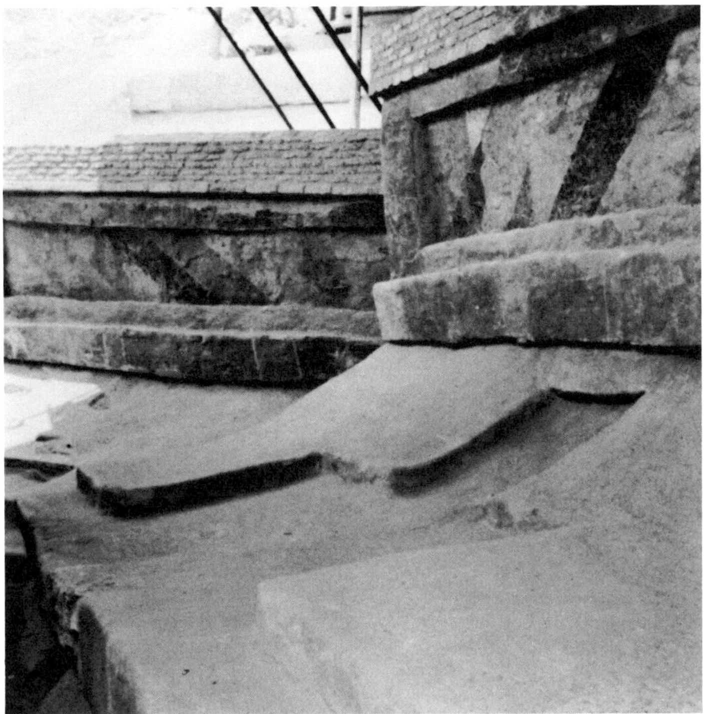

Fig. 11   Unique concave *taluds* from Patio of the Altars,
Cholula, Puebla. Photo by the author.

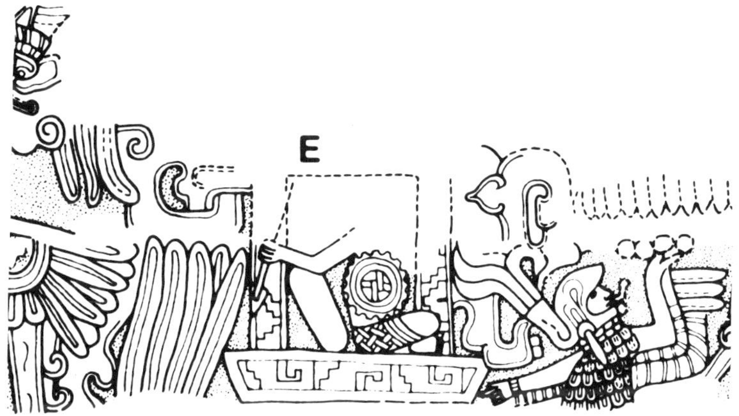

Fig. 12   Figure seated within a frame decorated with
step-pyramids, and on a platform embellished with step-
frets, Building Columns, Structure 2, Tajín Chico, Veracruz (after Kampen 1972: Fig. 32b, E).

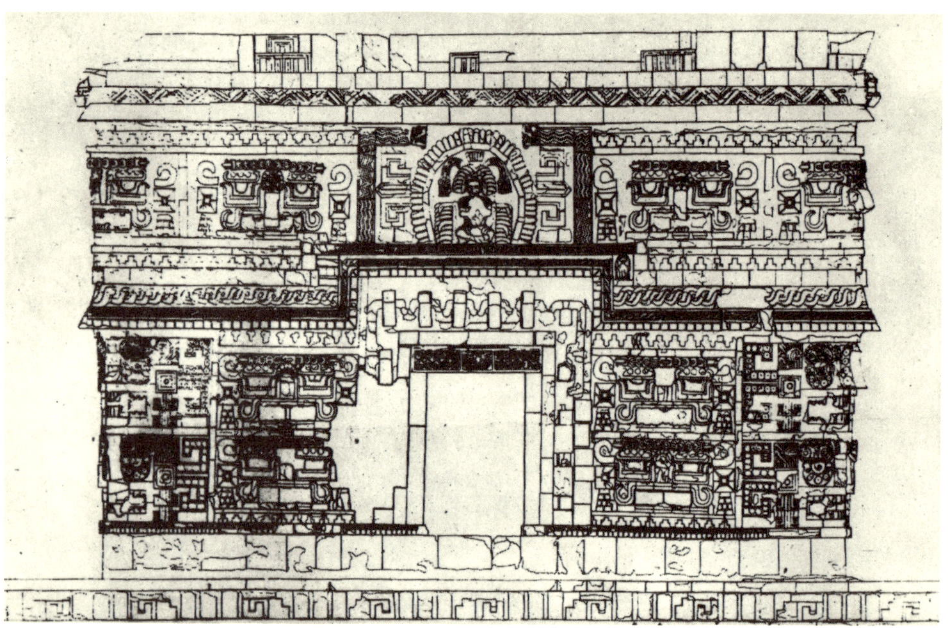

Fig. 13   Masks in association with sequences of step-frets and T-forms, East Annex, the Monjas (Nunnery), Chichén Itzá, Yucatán (after Marquina 1964: Fot. 415).

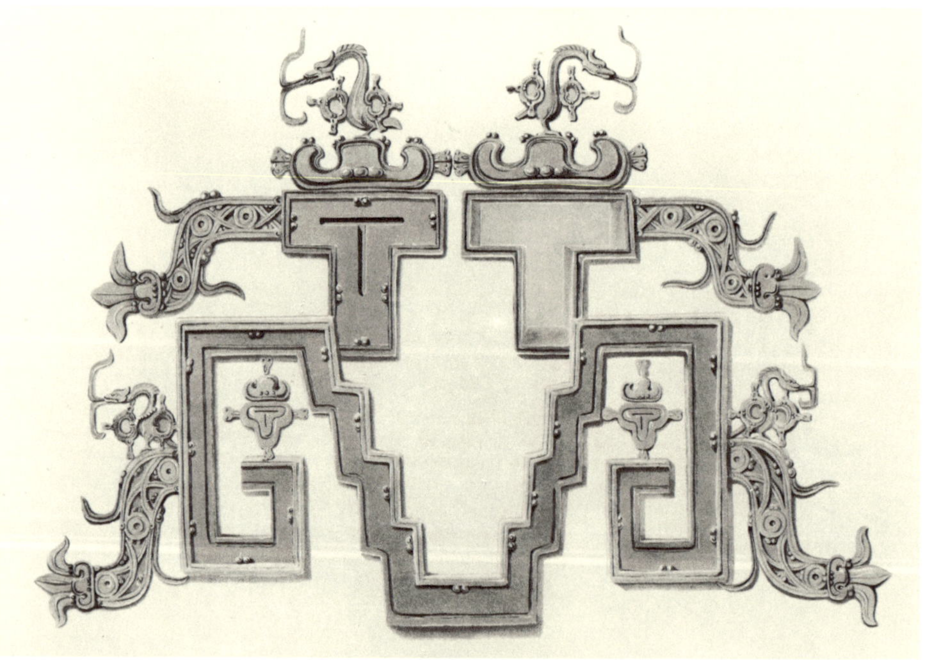

Fig. 14   T-motifs in association with opposing step-frets, rear wall, House B, Palace, Palenque, Chiapas (after Maudslay 1889–1902: Pl. 18).

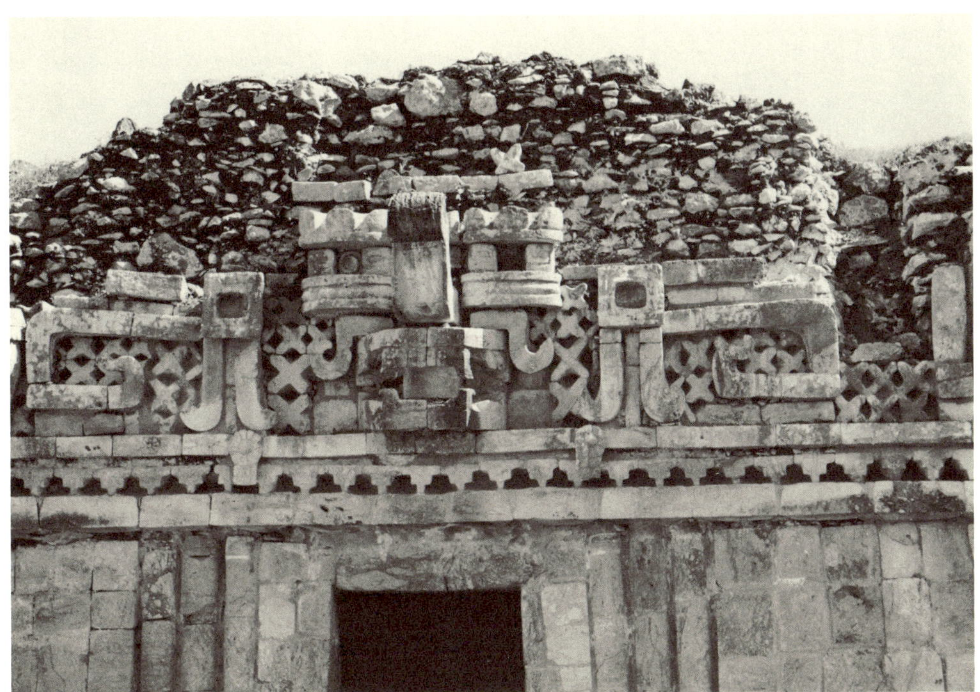

Fig. 15   Sequence of Ts in association with mosaic mask, East Wing, Palace, Labná, Yucatán. Photo by the author.

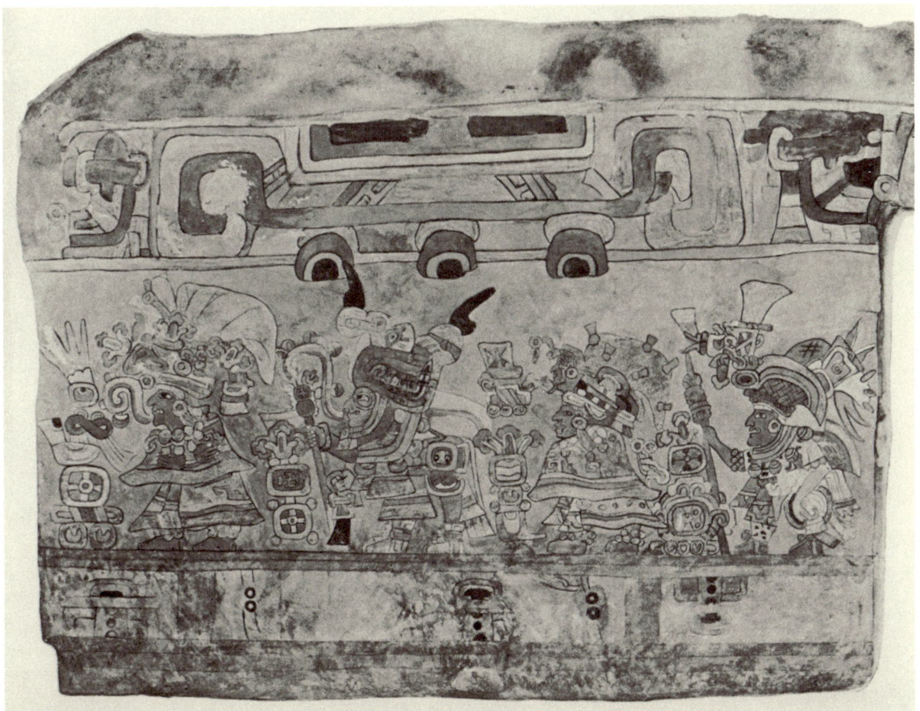

Fig. 16   Profile figures from Tomb 105, North Wall, Monte Albán, Oaxaca (after Caso 1938: Lám. IV).

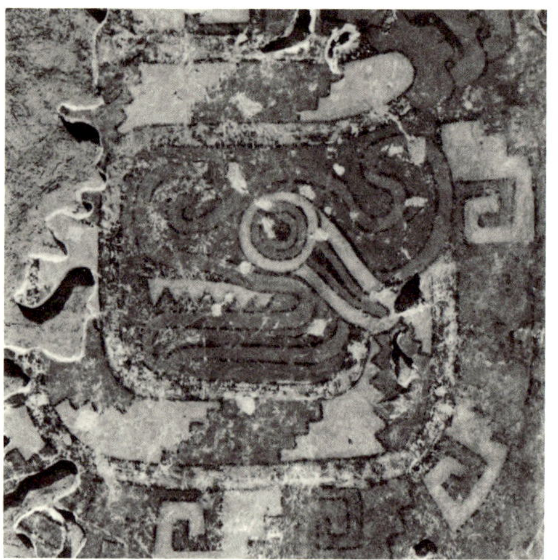

Fig. 17 Step-frets in association with a jaguar–serpent–bird, detail of Mural 2, Zone 5-A, Room 1, Teotihuacan, México (after Miller 1973: Fig. 103).

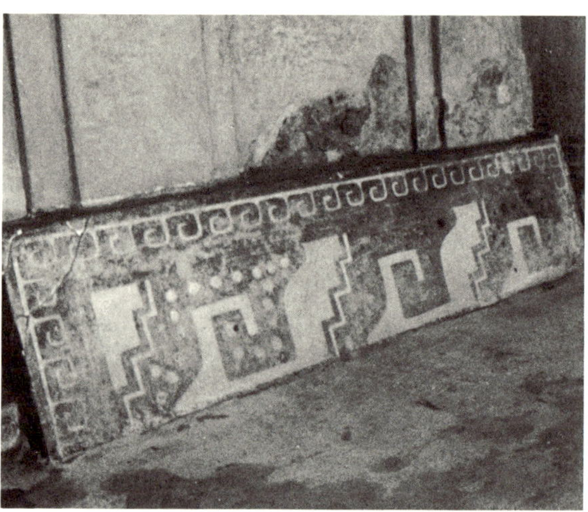

Fig. 18 Sequence of step-frets from the Palace of the Quetzal Butterfly, Teotihuacan, México. Photo by the author.

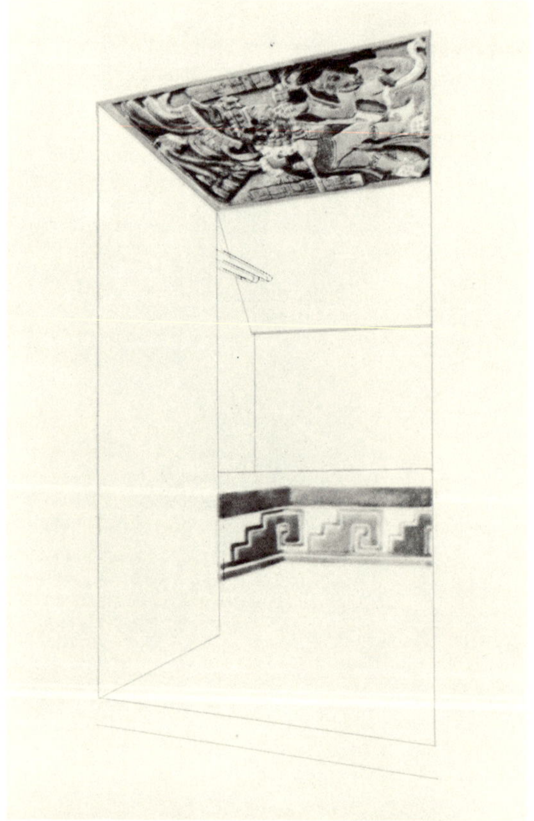

Fig. 19 Step-fret sequence on risers of platform in Room 1, Structure 1, Bonampak, Chiapas. Reproduction by Antonio Tejeda (after Ruppert, Thompson, and Proskouriakoff 1955: Fig. 27).

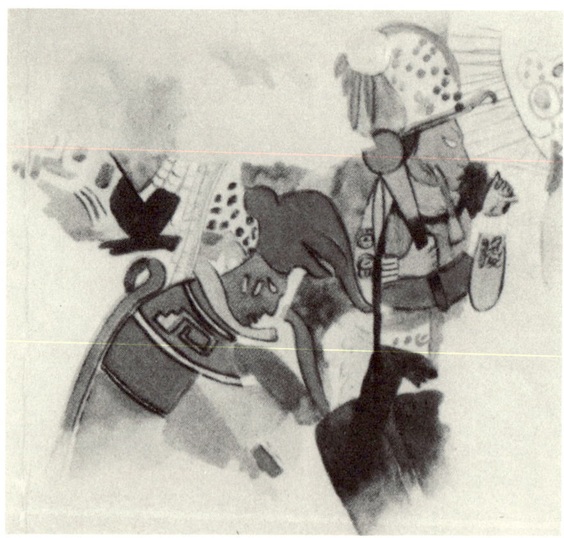

Fig. 20 Figure wearing a cloak adorned with a step-fret. Reproduction by Antonio Tejeda (after Ruppert, Thompson, and Proskouriakoff 1955: Fig. 28).

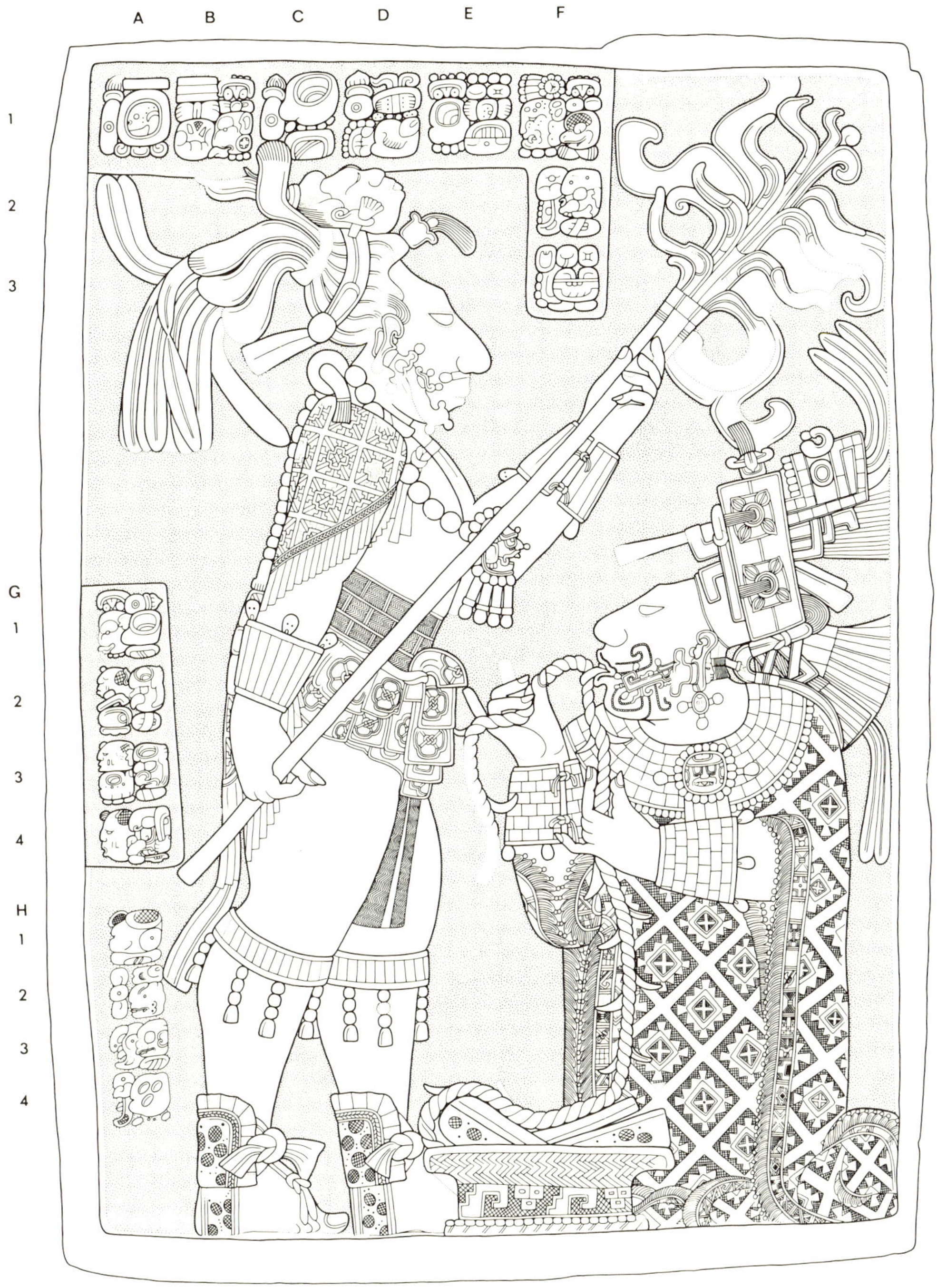

Fig. 21   Depiction of blood-letting ceremony; a basket decorated with a step-fret is also shown, Lintel 24, Structure 23, Yaxchilán, Chiapas. Drawing by Ian Graham (after Graham and von Euw 1977: 53).

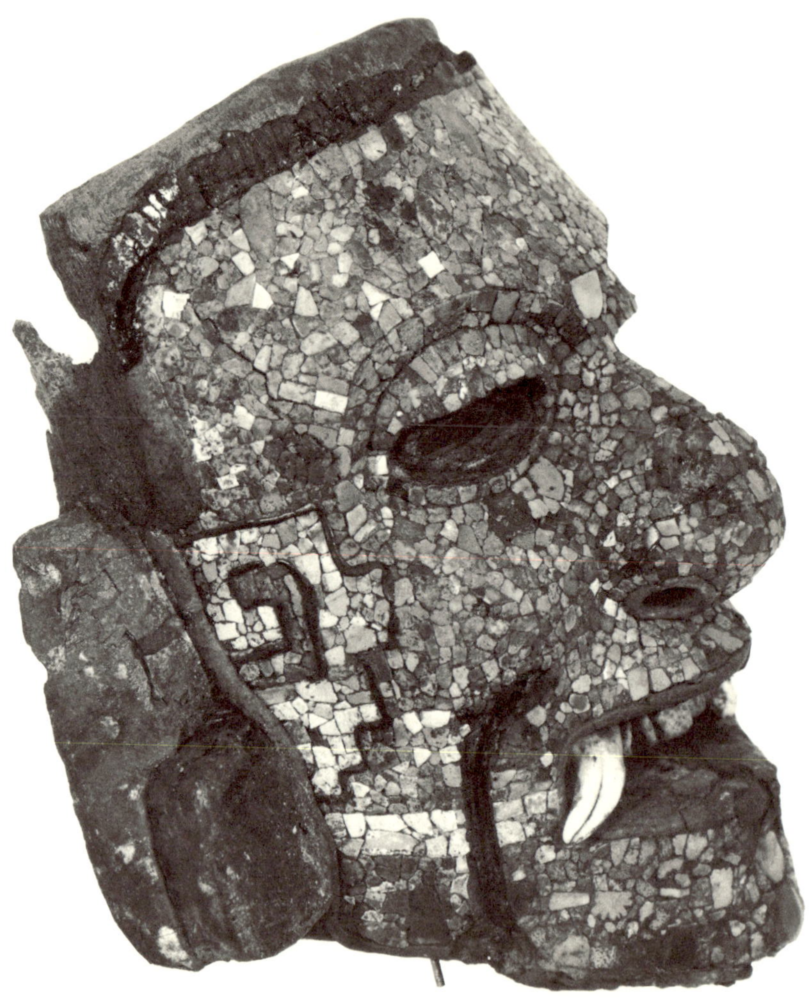

Fig. 22   Mask, turquoise mosaic on wood, with step-frets on both sides of the face. (Access. No. B-557.66.MAL) Dumbarton Oaks Collections, Washington, D.C.

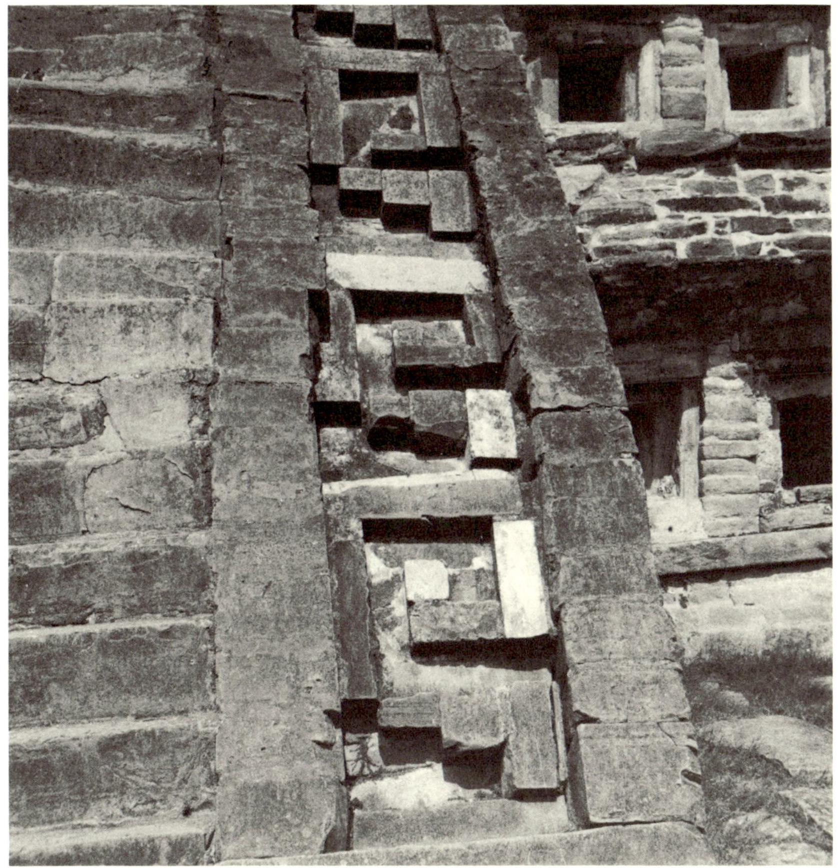

Fig. 23 Vertical sequences of step–frets, Pyramid of the Niches, El Tajín, Veracruz. Photo by the author.

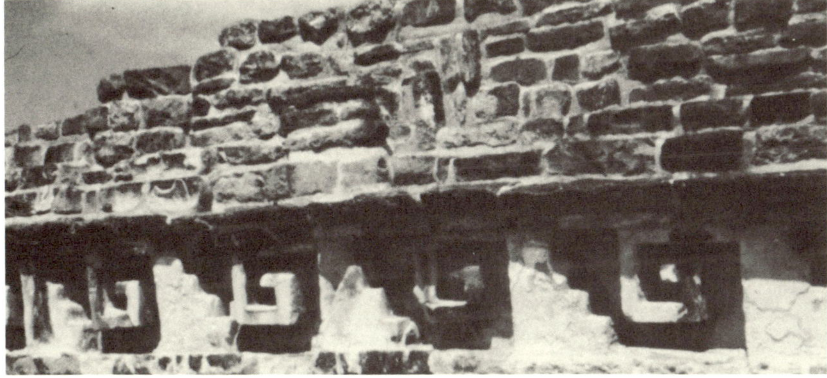

Fig. 24 Horizontal band of step–frets, Structure C, Tajín Chico, Veracruz. Photo by the author.

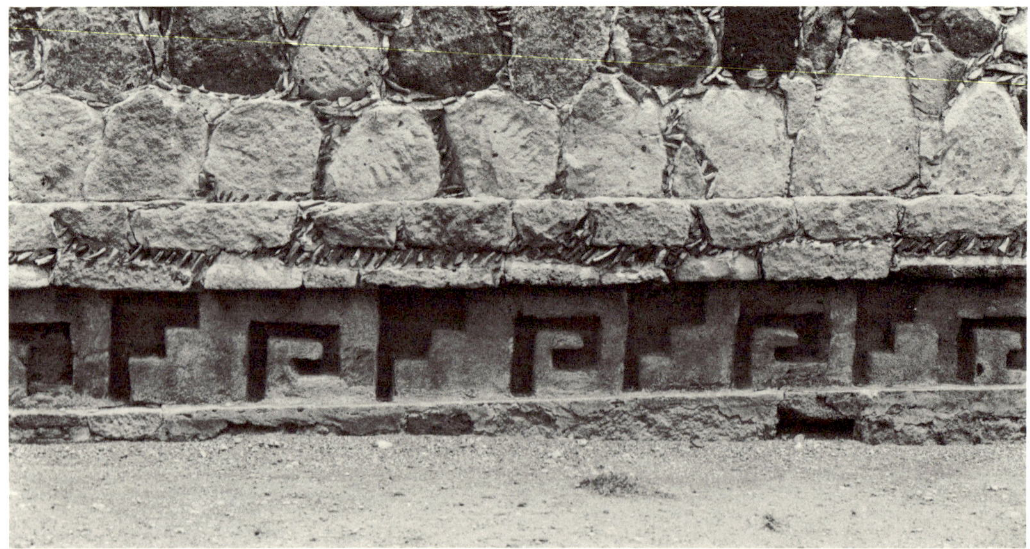

Fig. 25   Horizontal band of step–frets, rear of the major pyramid, Lambityeco, Oaxaca. Photo by the author.

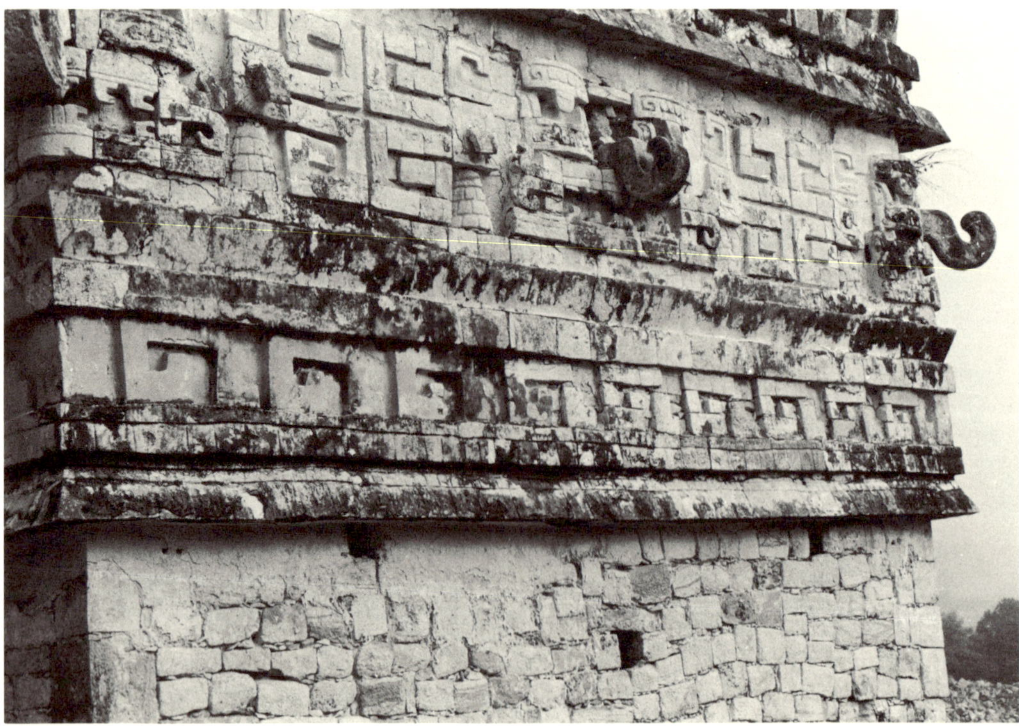

Fig. 26   Horizontal band of step–frets, Iglesia (Church), Chichén Itzá, Yucatán. Photo by the author.

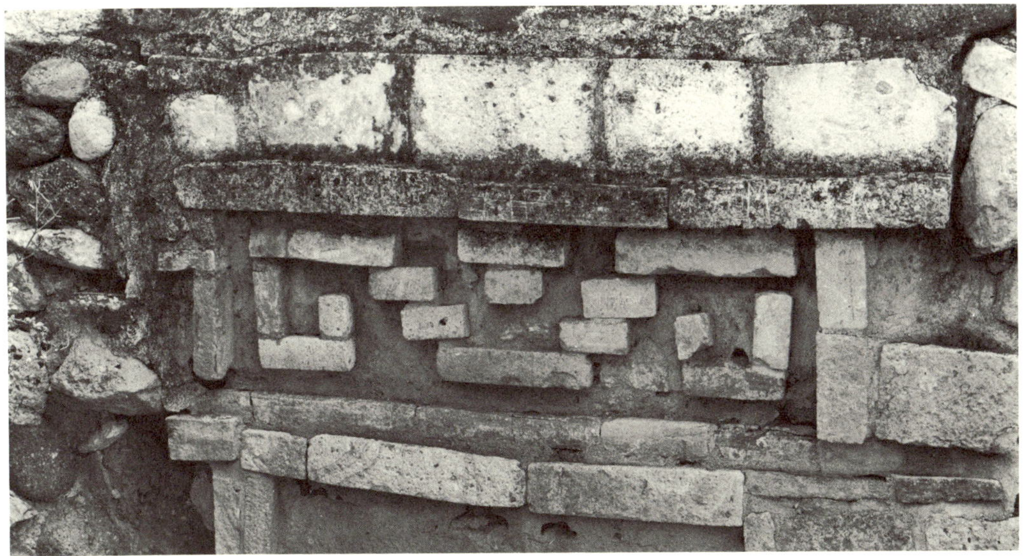

Fig. 27   Design in stone mosaics displaying bilateral horizontal symmetry, Tomb 11, Yagul, Oaxaca. Photo by the author.

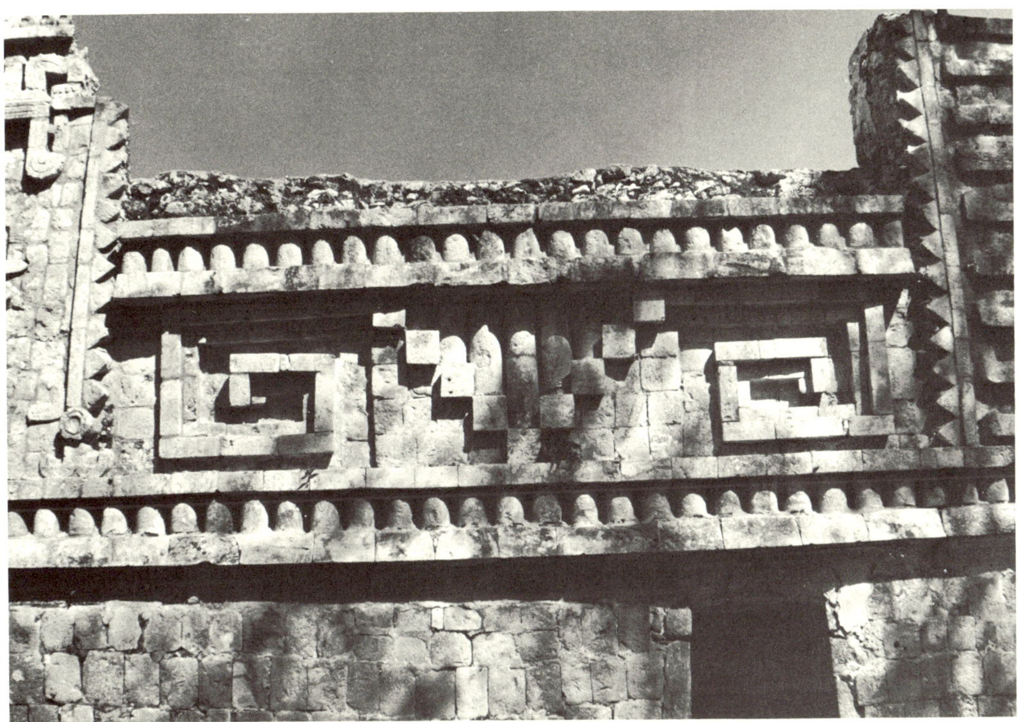

Fig. 28   Design displaying bilateral horizontal symmetry, Palace, Xlapac, Yucatán. Photo by the author.

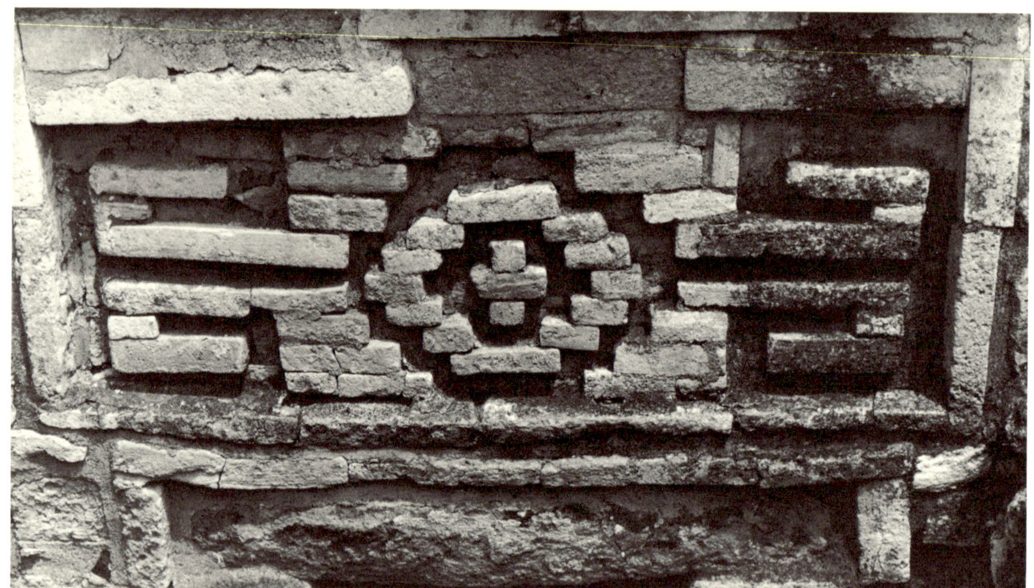

Fig. 29   Design displaying radial biaxial symmetry, Tomb 13, Mound 5-w, Yagul, Oaxaca.
Photo by the author.

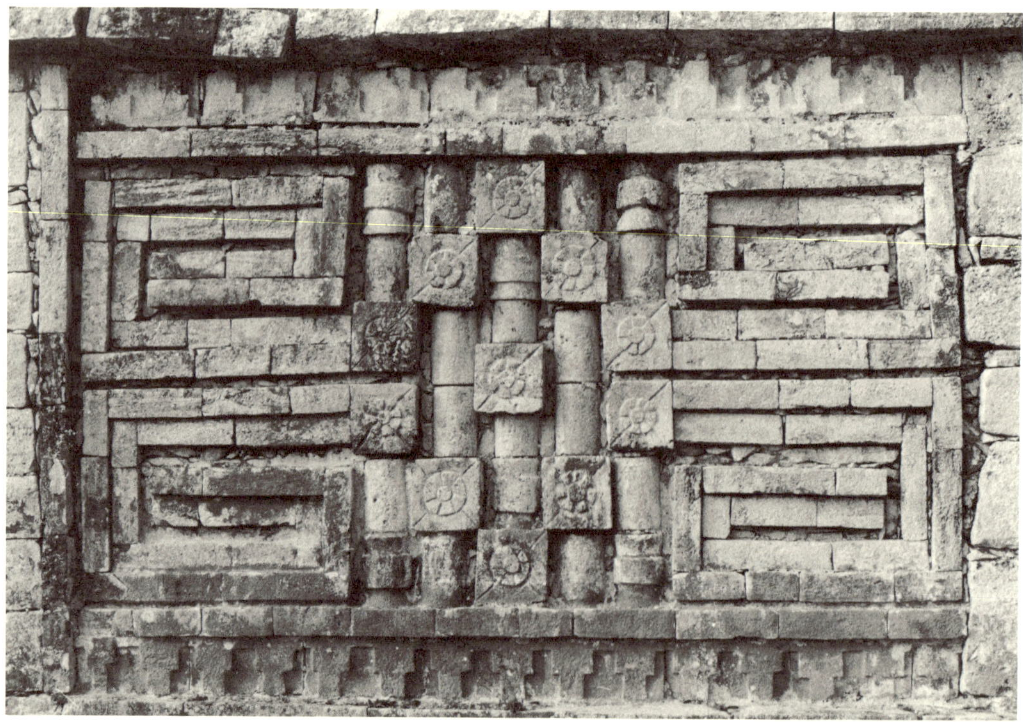

Fig. 30   Design displaying radial biaxial symmetry, second story, the Monjas (Nunnery),
Chichén Itzá, Yucatán. Photo by the author.

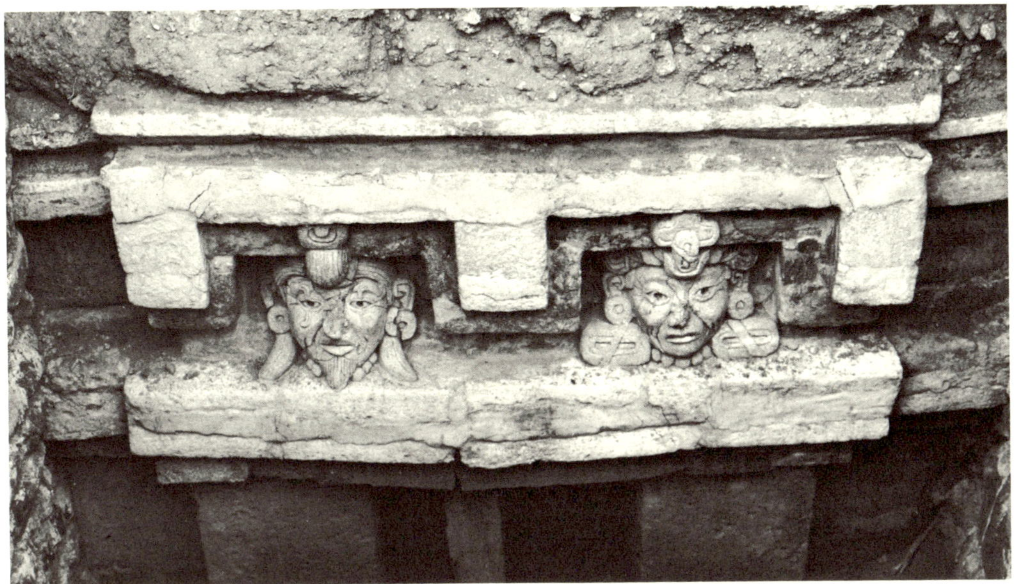

Fig. 31 Plaster "portrait heads" from Lambityeco, Oaxaca. Photo by the author.

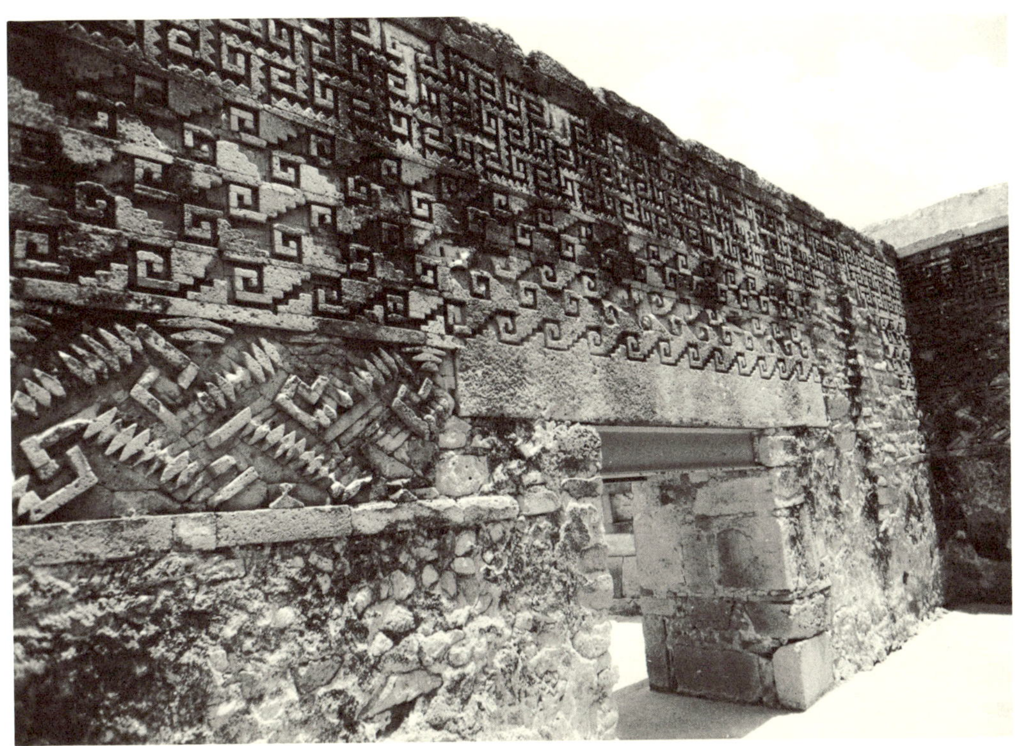

Fig. 32 Stone mosaic designs, Palace, Mitla, Oaxaca. Photo by the author.

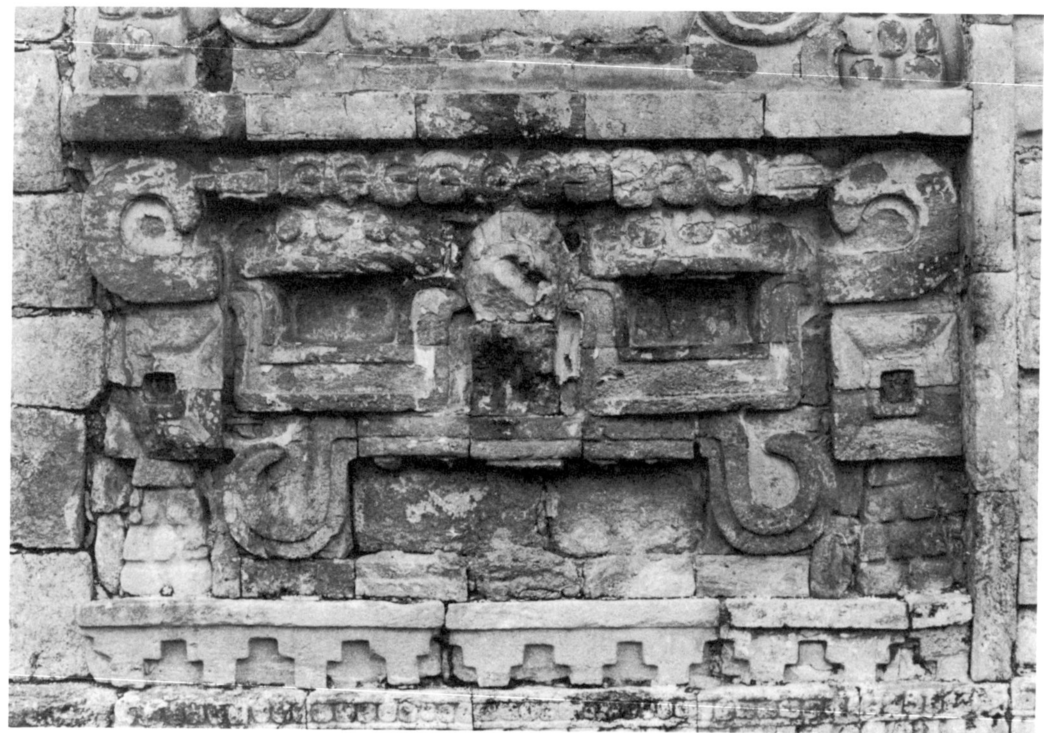

Fig. 33   Mosaic stone mask from East Annex, the Monjas (Nunnery), Chichén Itzá, Yucatán.
Photo by the author.

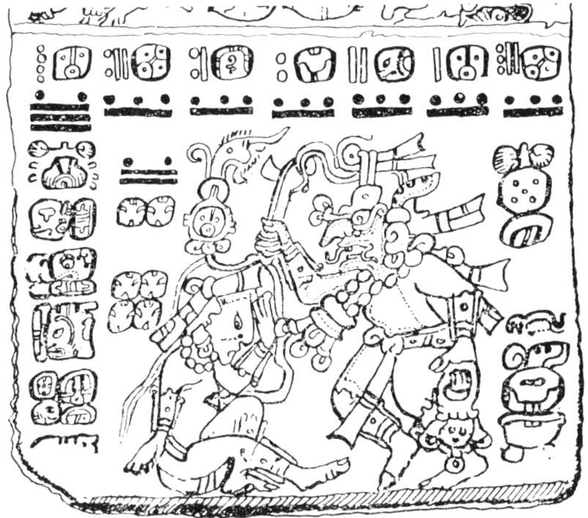

a Chac threatens the maize god.

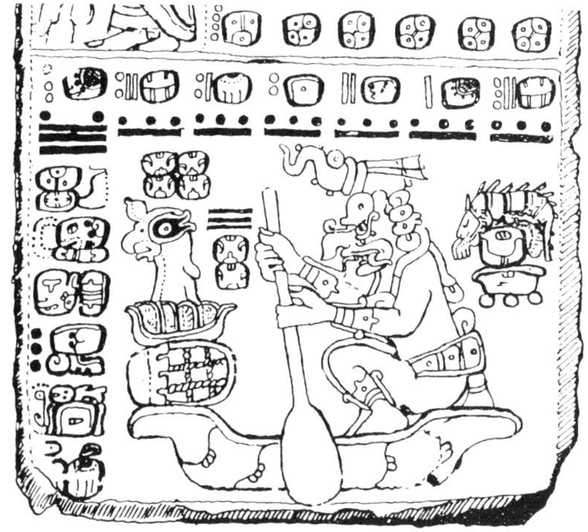

b Chac paddles a canoe.

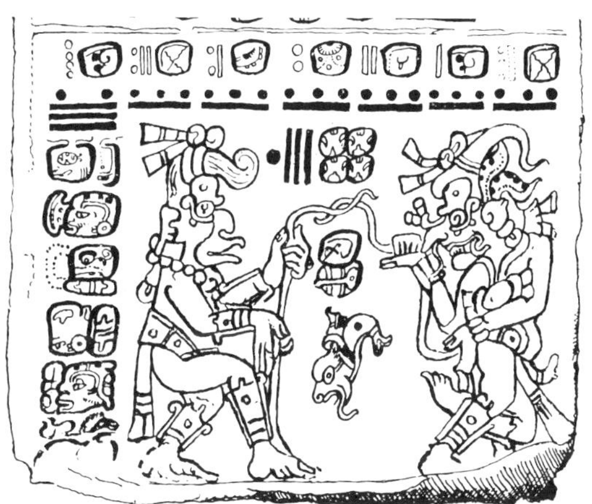

c Chac with another figure.

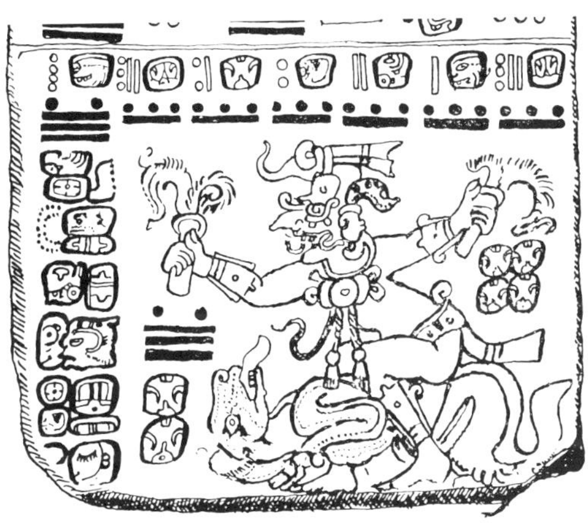

d Chac astride a dying deer.

Fig. 34   Chacs from the Codex Dresden (after Codex Dresden 1930: 94, 96, 98, 100, bottom third of pages).

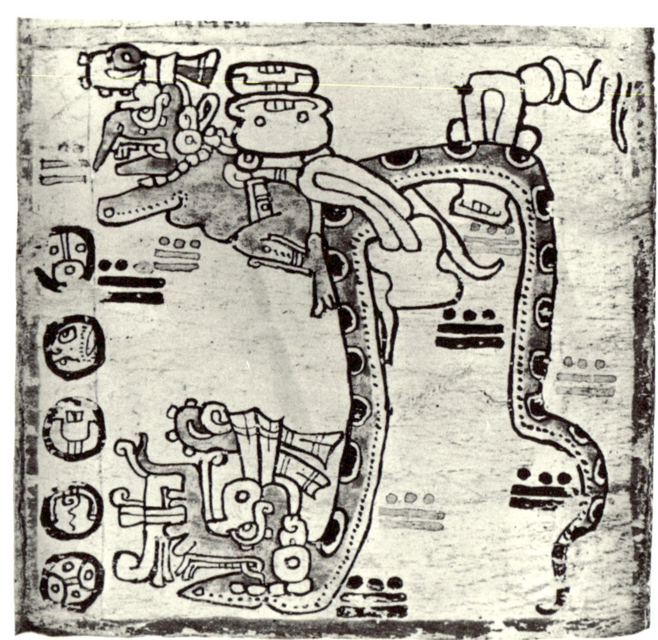

Fig. 35   Chac straddles the serpentine body of God K
(after Codex Madrid 1967: 31, lower half of page).

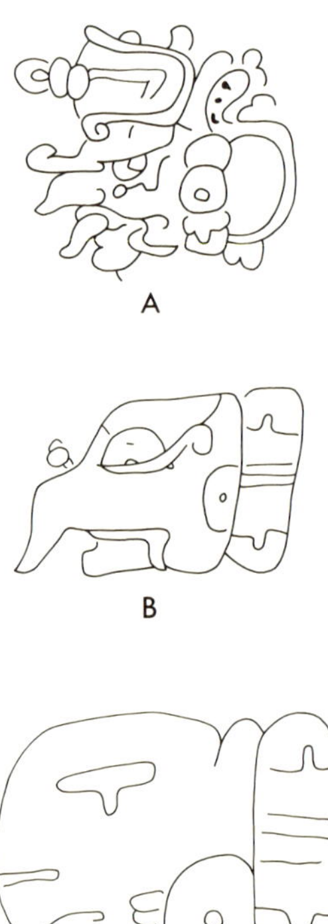

A

B

C

Fig. 36   Glyphs and representations of God B
from the Dresden and Madrid Codices.
Drawing by Whitney Powell.

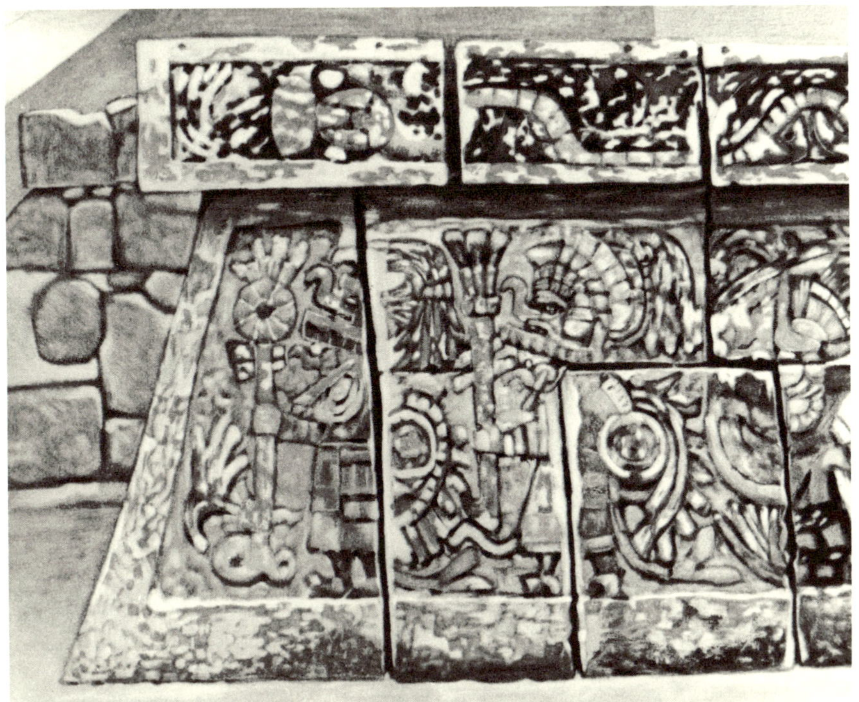

Fig. 37   Figures wearing long-nosed masks, northwest colonnade, south side, Temple of the Warriors, Chichén Itzá, Yucatán (after Morris, Charlot, and Morris 1931, II: Pl. 129).

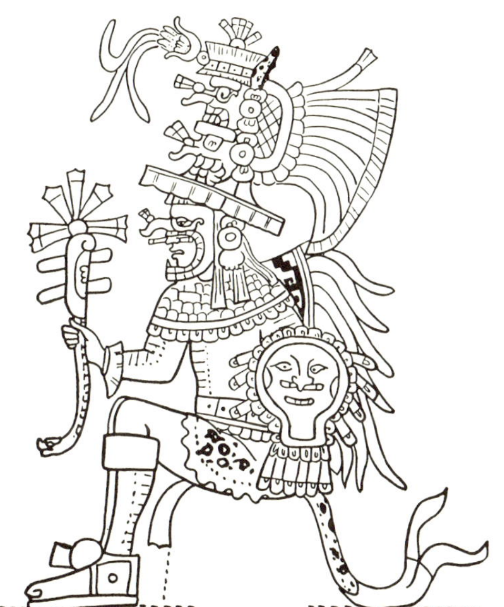

Fig. 38   Chac-Xib-Chac, God Impersonator, Temple of the Chac Mool, Chichén Itzá, Yucatán (after Roys 1967: 68, Fig. 2).

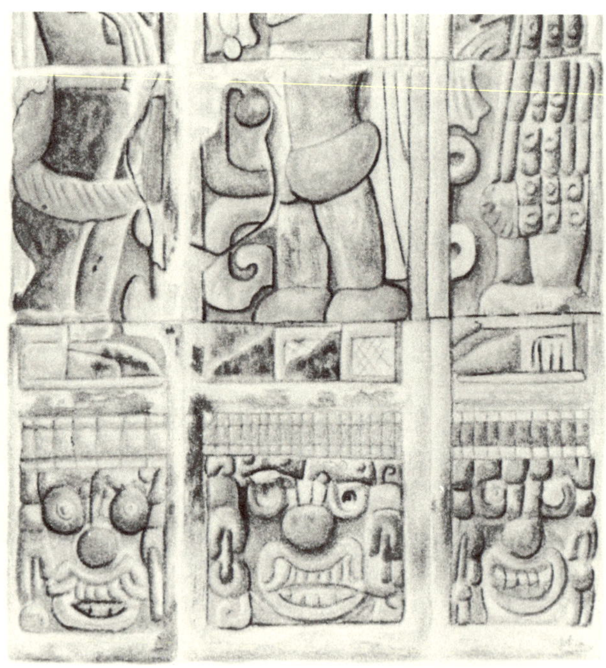

Fig. 39   Mask motifs at the base of Pilaster C, Temple of the Chac Mool, Chichén Itzá, Yucatán (after Morris, Charlot, and Morris 1931, II: Pl. 33).

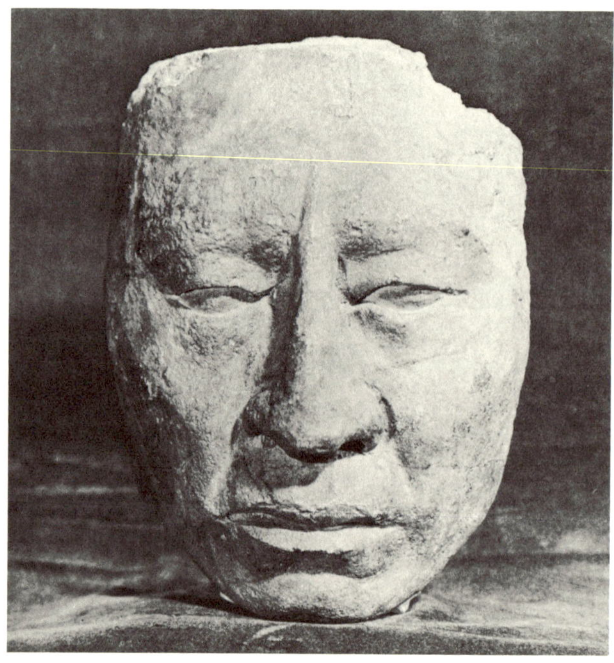

Fig. 40   Stucco "portrait" mask, Palenque, Chiapas (after Bernal 1969: 87).

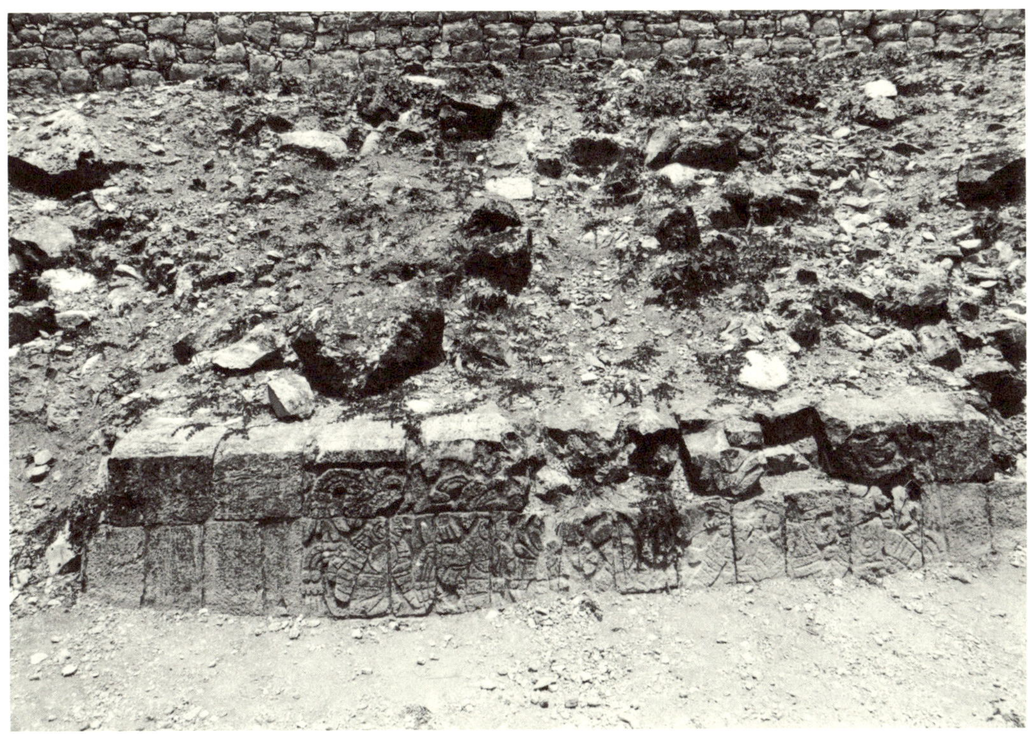

Fig. 41   Row of "Toltec-type" warriors, relief beneath the Casa Colorada (Red House),
Chichén Itzá, Yucatán. Photo by the author.

Bibliography

ANDREWS, E. WYLLYS, IV
1975   Progress Report on the 1960–1964 Field Seasons, National Geographic Society–Tulane University Dzibilchaltun Program. *In* Archaeological Investigations on the Yucatan Peninsula, pp. 23–67. *Middle American Research Institute, Tulane University*, Publication 31. New Orleans.

ANDREWS, E. WYLLYS, V
1979   Some Comments on Puuc Architecture of the Northern Yucatan Peninsula. *In* The Puuc: New Perspectives, Papers Presented at the Puuc Symposium, Central College, May, 1977 (Lawrence Mills, ed.), pp. 1–17. *Scholarly Studies in the Liberal Arts*, Publication No. 1, Central College, Pella, Iowa.

BALL, JOSEPH W.
1974   A Coordinate Approach to Northern Maya Prehistory: A.D. 700–1200. *American Antiquity*, vol. 39, no. 1, pp. 85–93.

BARRERA VASQUEZ, ALFREDO, and
SYLVANUS GRISWOLD MORLEY
1949   The Maya Chronicles. *Carnegie Institution of Washington, Contributions to American Anthropology and History, Publication 585*, vol. X, no. 48, pp. 1–85. Washington.

BECKER, MARSHALL JOSEPH
1975   Moieties in Ancient Mesoamerica: Inferences on Teotihuacán Social Structure, Part I. *American Indian Quarterly*, vol. 2, no. 3, pp. 217–236.

BERNAL, IGNACIO
1969   100 Great Masterpieces of the Mexican National Museum of Anthropology. Harry N. Abrams, Inc., New York.

BERNAL, IGNACIO, ROMÁN PIÑA CHAN, and
FERNANDO CÁMARA-BARBACHANO
1968   3000 Years of Art and Life in Mexico as seen in The Mexican National Museum of Anthropology. Harry N. Abrams, Inc., New York.

BEYER, HERMANN
1965   El Origen, Desarrollo y Significado de la Greca Escalonada. *El México Antiguo, Revista Internacional de Arqueología, Etnología, Folklore, Historia, Historia Antigua y Lingüística Mexicanas*, tomo X, pp. 53–104. (Originally published 1924.)

BRAINERD, GEORGE W.
1958   The Archaeological Ceramics of Yucatan. *Anthropological Records*, vol. 19. University of California Press, Berkeley.

CASO, ALFONSO
1938   Exploraciones en Oaxaca, Quinta y Sexta Temporadas, 1936–1937. *Instituto Panamericano de Geografía e Historia, Publicación número 34*, México.
1965   Sculpture and Mural Painting in Oaxaca. *In* Handbook of Middle American Indians (Robert Wauchope, ed.), vol. 3, part 2, pp. 849–870. University of Texas Press, Austin.

CASO, ALFONSO, and IGNACIO BERNAL
1952   Urnas de Oaxaca. *Memorias del Instituto Nacional de Antropología e Historia*, II. Secretaría de Educación Pública, México.

CASO, ALFONSO, IGNACIO BERNAL, and
JORGE R. ACOSTA
1967   La Cerámica de Monte Albán. *Memorias del Instituto Nacional de Antropología e Historia*, XIII. Secretaría de Educación Pública, México.

CHARNAY, DÉSIRÉ
1888   The Ancient Cities of the New World, being Voyages and Explorations in Mexico and Central America from 1857–1882. Harper and Brothers, New York.

CODEX DRESDEN
1930   Códice de Dresden, Procedente del Petén, Guatemala. *In* Códices Mayas (J. Antonio and Carlos A. Villacorta). Tipografía Nacional, Guatemala.

CODEX FEJÉRVÁRY–MAYER
1971   Codex Fejérváry–Mayer. City of Liverpool Museums. Introduction, C. A. Burland. Akademische Druck- und Verlagsanstalt, Graz, Austria.

CODEX MADRID
1967   Codex Tro-Cortesianus (Codex Madrid). Museo de América, Madrid. Introduction and Summary, F. Anders. Akademische Druck- und Verlagsanstalt, Graz, Austria.

CODEX MAGLIABECHIANO
1970   Codex Magliabechiano. Biblioteca Nazionale Centrale de Firenze. Introduction and Summary, Ferdinand Anders. Akademische Druck- und Verlagsanstalt, Graz, Austria.

COE, MICHAEL D.
1965   A Model of Ancient Community Structure in the Maya Lowlands. *Southwestern Journal of Anthropology*, vol. 21, no. 2, pp. 97–114.
1972   Olmec Jaguars and Olmec Kings. *In* The Cult of the Feline: A Conference in Pre-Columbian

Iconography (Elizabeth P. Benson, ed.), pp. 1–18. Dumbarton Oaks Research Library and Collections, Washington.

1973 The Maya Scribe and His World. The Grolier Club, New York.

1974 A Carved Wooden Box from the Classic Maya Civilization. *In* Primera Mesa Redonda de Palenque, Part II: A Conference on the Art, Iconography, and Dynastic History of Palenque; Palenque, Chiapas, Mexico. December 14–22, 1973 (Merle Greene Robertson, ed.), pp. 51–58. The Robert Louis Stevenson School, Pebble Beach.

1975 Three Maya Figurines from Jaina Island. *Yale University Art Gallery Bulletin*, vol. 35, no. 2, pp. 24–25. New Haven.

COE, MICHAEL D., and ELIZABETH P. BENSON

1966 Three Maya Relief Panels at Dumbarton Oaks. *Studies in Pre-Columbian Art and Archaeology*, no. 2. Dumbarton Oaks, Washington.

CULBERT, T. PATRICK (ed.)

1973 The Classic Maya Collapse. School of American Research, University of New Mexico Press, Albuquerque.

DAVIES, NIGEL

1977 The Toltecs until the Fall of Tula. University of Oklahoma Press, Norman.

DIEHL, RICHARD A. (ed.)

1974 Studies of Ancient Tollan: A Report of the University of Missouri Tula Archaeological Project. *University of Missouri Monographs in Anthropology*, no. 1. University of Missouri, Columbia.

DIEHL, RICHARD A., and ROBERT A. BENFER

1975 Tollan: The Toltec Capital. *Archaeology*, vol. 28, no. 2, pp. 112–124.

DUMBARTON OAKS COLLECTIONS

1969 Supplement to the Handbook of the Robert Woods Bliss Collection of Pre-Columbian Art. Dumbarton Oaks, Washington.

FEWKES, J. WALTER

1894 A Study of Certain Figures in a Maya Codex. *American Anthropologist*, vol. VII, no. 3, pp. 260–274.

FLANNERY, KENT V., and JOYCE MARCUS

1976 Formative Oaxaca and the Zapotec Cosmos. *American Scientist*, vol. 64, no. 4, pp. 374–383.

FONCERRADA DE MOLINA, MARTA

1965 La Escultura Arquitectónica de Uxmal. Instituto de Investigaciones Estéticas, Universidad Nacional Autónoma de México, XX. México.

GARCÍA PAYON, JOSÉ

1951 La Pirámide del Tajín: Estudio Analítico. *Cuadernos Americanos*, Año X, vol. LX, no. 6, Noviembre–Diciembre, pp. 153–157. México.

1971 Archaeology of Central Veracruz. *In* Handbook of Middle American Indians (Robert Wauchope, ed.), vol. 11, part 2, pp. 505–542. University of Texas Press, Austin.

1973 La Ciudad Sagrada de Hurakán. *In* Los Enigmas de El Tajín. Instituto Nacional de Antropología e Historia, Colección Científica, Arqueología, no. 3, pp. 5–30. México.

GLASS, JOHN B., and DONALD ROBERTSON

1975 A Census of Native Middle American Pictorial Manuscripts. *In* Handbook of Middle American Indians (Robert Wauchope, ed.), vol. 14, part 3, pp. 81–252. University of Texas Press, Austin.

GRAHAM, IAN, and ERIC VON EUW

1977 Corpus of Maya Hieroglyphic Inscriptions, vol. 3, pt. 1, Yaxchilan. Peabody Museum of Archaeology and Ethnology, Harvard University, Cambridge.

GRAHAM, JOHN A.

1973 Aspects of Non-Classic Presences in the Inscriptions and Sculptural Art of Seibal. *In* The Classic Maya Collapse (T. Patrick Culbert, ed.), pp. 207–219. University of New Mexico Press, Albuquerque.

GREENE, MERLE, ROBERT L. RANDS, and JOHN A. GRAHAM

1972 Maya Sculpture from the Southern Lowlands, the Highlands, and Pacific Piedmont: Guatemala, Mexico, Honduras. Lederer, Street, and Zeus, Berkeley.

GREENE ROBERTSON, MERLE, MARJORIE S. ROSENBLUM SCANDIZZO, and JOHN R. SCANDIZZO

1976 Physical Deformities in the Ruling Lineage of Palenque and the Dynastic Implications. *In* The Art, Iconography & Dynastic History of Palenque, Part III. Proceedings of the Segunda Mesa Redonda de Palenque, December 14–21, 1974, Palenque (Merle Greene Robertson, ed.), pp. 59–86. The Robert Louis Stevenson School, Pebble Beach.

GREG, ROBERT PHILIPS

1882 The Fret or Key Ornamentation in Mexico and Peru. *Archaeologia*, vol. XLVII, pp. 157–160.

GRIEDER, TERENCE

1975 The Interpretation of Ancient Symbols. *American Anthropologist*, vol. 77, no. 4, pp. 849–855.

HAVILAND, WILLIAM A.

1975 The Ancient Maya and the Evolution of Urban Society. Museum of Anthropology *Miscellaneous*

Series No. 37, University of Northern Colorado, Greeley.

1978 The Rise of the Maya (book review of The Origins of Maya Civilization, edited by Richard E. W. Adams). *Science*, vol. 199, pp. 761–762.

HOLMES, WILLIAM H.

1895– Archaeological Studies among the Ancient
1897 Cities of Mexico, Part I. *Field Columbian Museum, Publication 8, Anthropological Series*, vol. I, no. I. Chicago.

HVIDTFELDT, ARILD

1958 Teotl and Ixiptlatli: Some Central Conceptions in Ancient Mexican Religion. Munksgaard, Copenhagen.

INGHAM, JOHN M.

1971 Time and Space in Ancient Mexico: The Symbolic Dimensions of Clanship. *Man*, New Series, vol. 6, no. 4, pp. 615–629.

INSTITUTO NACIONAL DE ANTROPOLOGÍA
E HISTORIA

1966 Noticias de los Museos; Pieza del Mes, Septiembre. *Boletín*, no. 25, pp. 39–41. México.

JIMÉNEZ MORENO, WIGBERTO

1966 Mesoamerica before the Toltecs. *In* Ancient Oaxaca, Discoveries in Mexican Archaeology and History (John Paddock, ed.), pp. 1–82. Stanford University Press, Stanford.

JORALEMON, DAVID

1974 Ritual Blood-Sacrifice among the Ancient Maya: Part I. *In* Primera Mesa Redonda de Palenque, Part II: A Conference on the Art, Iconography, and Dynastic History of Palenque; Palenque, Chiapas, Mexico. December 14–22, 1973 (Merle Greene Robertson, ed.), pp. 59–76. The Robert Louis Stevenson School, Pebble Beach.

KAMPEN, MICHAEL EDWIN

1972 The Sculptures of El Tajín, Veracruz, México. University of Florida Press, Gainesville.

KELLEY, DAVID H.

1968 Kakupacal and the Itzas. *Estudios de Cultura Maya*, vol. VII, pp. 255–268. Universidad Nacional Autónoma de México, México.

KUBLER, GEORGE

1967 The Iconography of the Art of Teotihuacán. *Studies in Pre-Columbian Art and Archaeology*, no. 4 (Elizabeth P. Benson, ed.). Dumbarton Oaks, Washington.

1969 Studies in Classic Maya Iconography. *Memoirs of the Connecticut Academy of Arts & Sciences*, vol. XVIII. New Haven.

1973 Science and Humanism among Americanists. *In* The Iconography of Middle American Sculpture, pp. 163–167. The Metropolitan Museum of Art, New York.

1975a History—or Anthropology—of Art? *Critical Inquiry*, vol. I, no. 4, pp. 757–767.

1975b The Art and Architecture of Ancient America: The Mexican, Maya, and Andean Peoples. Penguin Books, Baltimore. (Originally published 1962.)

LOTHROP, SAMUEL KIRKLAND

1952 Metals from the Cenote of Sacrifice, Chichen Itza, Yucatan. *Memoirs of the Peabody Museum of Archaeology and Ethnology, Harvard University*, vol. X, no. 2. Cambridge.

LUMBRERAS, LUÍS G.

1974 The Peoples and Cultures of Ancient Peru. Translated by Betty J. Meggers. Smithsonian Institution Press, Washington.

LUMHOLTZ, CARL

1909 A Remarkable Ceremonial Vessel from Cholula, Mexico. *American Anthropologist*, vol. II, pp. 199–201.

MALER, TEOBERT

1901 Researches in the Central Portion of the Usumatsintla Valley: Report of Explorations for the Museum, 1898–1900. *Memoirs of the Peabody Museum of American Archaeology and Ethnology, Harvard University*, vol. II. Cambridge.

MARQUINA, IGNACIO

1951 Arquitectura Prehispánica. *Memorias del Instituto Nacional de Antropología e Historia*, I. Secretaría de Educación Pública, México.

MAUDSLAY, A. P.

1889– Biologia Centrali-Americana: Archaeology, vol.
1902 IV. R. H. Porter and Dulau & Co., London.

MEISS, MILLARD

1973 Painting in Florence and Siena after the Black Death: The Arts, Religion and Society in the Mid-Fourteenth Century. Icon Editions, Harper & Row, New York. (Originally published 1951, Princeton University Press.)

MILLER, ARTHUR G.

1973 The Mural Painting of Teotihuacán. Dumbarton Oaks, Washington.

MILLON, CLARA

1972 The History of Mural Art at Teotihuacan. *In* Teotihuacan, *XI Mesa Redonda*, pp. 1–16. Sociedad Mexicana de Antropología, Mexico.

1973 Painting, Writing, and Polity in Teotihuacan, Mexico. *American Antiquity*, vol. 38, no. 3, pp. 294–314.

MILLON, RENÉ (ed.)

1973 Urbanization at Teotihuacán, Mexico, Volume One: The Teotihuacán Map, Part One: Text. University of Texas Press, Austin.

MOLLOY, JOHN P., and WILLIAM L. RATHJE

1974 Sexploitation among the Late Classic Maya. *In* Mesoamerican Archaeology: New Approaches (Norman Hammond, ed.), pp. 431–444. Proceedings of a Symposium on Mesoamerican Archaeology Held by the University of Cambridge Centre of Latin American Studies, August 1972. University of Texas Press, Austin.

MORLEY, SYLVANUS GRISWOLD

1937– The Inscriptions of Peten. *Carnegie Institution*
1938 *of Washington, Publication no. 437*, vol. 5, part 1. Washington.

MORRIS, EARL H., JEAN CHARLOT, and ANN AXTELL MORRIS

1931 The Temple of the Warriors at Chichen Itza, Yucatan. *Carnegie Institution of Washington, Publication 406*, 2 vols. Washington.

MUNN, NANCY

1973 Walbiri Iconography: Graphic Representation and Cultural Symbolism in a Central Australian Society. Cornell University Press, Ithaca.

NICHOLSON, HENRY B.

1966 The Mixteca-Puebla Concept in Mesoamerican Archeology: A Re-examination. International Congress of Anthropological Sciences; *reprinted in* Ancient Mesoamerica: Selected Readings (John A. Graham, ed.), pp. 258–263. Peek Publications, Palo Alto.

1971 Major Sculpture in Pre-Hispanic Central Mexico. *In* Handbook of Middle American Indians (Robert Wauchope, ed.), vol. 10, part 1, pp. 92–134. University of Texas Press, Austin.

1976 Preclassic Mesoamerican Iconography from the Perspective of the Postclassic: Problems in Interpretational Analysis. *In* Origins of Religious Art & Iconography in Preclassic Mesoamerica (H. B. Nicholson, ed.), pp. 157–175. UCLA Latin American Center–Ethnic Arts Council of Los Angeles, Los Angeles.

PADDOCK, JOHN

1978 The Middle Classic Period in Oaxaca. *In* Middle Classic Mesoamerica: A.D. 400–700 (Esther Pasztory, ed.), pp. 45–62. Columbia University Press, New York.

n.d. Mesoamérica no es el Valle de México. Paper delivered at the XLI Congreso Internacional de Americanistas, México, September 2–7, 1974.

PADDOCK, JOHN (ed.)

1966 Ancient Oaxaca: Discoveries in Mexican Archeology and History. Stanford University Press, Stanford.

PARRY, FRANCIS

1894 The Sacred Symbols and Numbers of Aboriginal America in Ancient and Modern Times. *Bulletin of the American Geographical Society*, pp. 1–46. (Reprint 1976: Frontier Book Company, Fort Davis, Texas.)

PARSONS, LEE ALLEN

1969 Bilbao, Guatemala: An Archaeological Study of the Pacific Coast Cotzumalhuapa Region. *Milwaukee Public Museum, Publications in Anthropology* 12, vol. 2. Milwaukee.

POLLOCK, HARRY E. D.

1965 Architecture of the Maya Lowlands. *In* Handbook of Middle American Indians (Robert Wauchope, ed.), vol. 2, part 1, pp. 378–440. University of Texas Press, Austin.

POZORSKI, THOMAS

1975 El Complejo Caballo Muerto y los Frisos de Barro de la Huaca de los Reyes. *Revista del Museo Nacional*, tomo XLI, pp. 211–251. Museo Nacional de la Cultura Peruana, Lima.

PROSKOURIAKOFF, TATIANA

1955 The Death of a Civilization. *Scientific American*, vol. 192, no. 5, pp. 82–88.

1961 Portraits of Women in Maya Art. *In* Essays in Pre-Columbian Art and Archaeology (S. K. Lothrop *et al.*, eds.), pp. 81–99. Harvard University Press, Cambridge.

1963 Historical Data in the Inscriptions of Yaxchilan, Part 1: The Reign of Shield Jaguar. *Estudios de Cultura Maya*, vol. III, pp. 149–167. Universidad Nacional Autónoma de México, México.

1970 On Two Inscriptions at Chichen Itza. *In* Monographs and Papers in Maya Archaeology (William R. Bullard, Jr., ed.), *Papers of the Peabody Museum of Archaeology and Ethnology, Harvard University*, vol. 61, part v, no. 2, pp. 457–467. Cambridge.

1974 Jades from the Cenote of Sacrifice, Chichen Itza, Yucatan. *Memoirs of the Peabody Museum of Archaeology and Ethnology, Harvard University*, vol. 10, no. 1. Cambridge.

PROSKOURIAKOFF, TATIANA, and J. ERIC S. THOMPSON

1947 Maya Calendar Round Dates Such as 9 Ahau 17 Mol. *Carnegie Institution of Washington, Division of Historical Research, Notes on Middle American*

Archaeology and Ethnology, vol. 3, no. 79, pp. 143–150. Cambridge.

PULESTON, DENNIS E.

1977 The Art and Archaeology of Hydraulic Agriculture in the Maya Lowlands. *In* Social Process in Maya Prehistory: Studies in Honour of Sir Eric Thompson (Norman Hammond, ed.), pp. 449–467. Academic Press, London.

RABIN, EMILY

1970 The Lambityeco Friezes: Notes on Their Content, with an Appendix on C14 Dates. *Bulletin of Oaxaca Studies*, no. 33. Mitla.

RANDS, ROBERT

1973 A Chronological Framework for Palenque. *In* Primera Mesa Redonda de Palenque, Part I: A Conference on the Art, Iconography, and Dynastic History of Palenque; Palenque, Chiapas, Mexico. December 14–22, 1973 (Merle Greene Robertson, ed.), pp. 35–39. The Robert Louis Stevenson School, Pebble Beach.

RICKARDS, CONSTANTINE GEORGE

1910 The Ruins of Mexico, vol. 1. H. E. Shrimpton, London.

ROWE, JOHN HOWLAND, and DOROTHY MENZEL (eds.)

1967 Peruvian Archaeology: Selected Readings. Peek Publications, Palo Alto.

ROYS, RALPH L.

1967 The Book of Chilam Balam of Chumayel. University of Oklahoma Press, Norman. (Originally published 1933.)

ROYS, RALPH L. (trans. and ed.)

1965 Ritual of the Bacabs. University of Oklahoma Press, Norman.

RUPPERT, KARL, J. ERIC S. THOMPSON, and TATIANA PROSKOURIAKOFF

1955 Bonampak, Chiapas, Mexico. *Carnegie Institution of Washington, Publication 602*. Washington.

SABLOFF, JEREMY

1977 Old Myths, New Myths: The Role of Sea Traders in the Development of Ancient Maya Civilization. *In* The Sea in the Pre-Columbian World: A Conference at Dumbarton Oaks, October 26th and 27th, 1974 (Elizabeth P. Benson, ed.), pp. 67–96. Dumbarton Oaks Research Library and Collections, Washington.

SABLOFF, JEREMY A., and WILLIAM L. RATHJE

1975 The Rise of a Maya Merchant Class. *Scientific American*, vol. 233, no. 4, pp. 72–82.

SCHELE, LINDA

1974 Observations on the Cross Motif at Palenque. *In* Primera Mesa Redonda de Palenque, Part I: A Conference on the Art, Iconography, and Dynastic History of Palenque; Palenque, Chiapas, Mexico. December 14–22, 1973 (Merle Greene Robertson, ed.), pp. 41–61. The Robert Louis Stevenson School, Pebble Beach.

1976 Accession Iconography of Chan-Bahlum in the Group of the Cross at Palenque. *In* The Art, Iconography, and Dynastic History of Palenque, Part III. Proceedings of the Segunda Mesa Redonda de Palenque, December 14–21, 1974, Palenque (Merle Greene Robertson, ed.), pp. 9–34. The Robert Louis Stevenson School, Pebble Beach.

SCHELLHAS, PAUL

1904 Representations of Deities of the Maya Manuscripts. *Papers of the Peabody Museum of American Archaeology and Ethnology, Harvard University*, vol. IV, no. 1. Cambridge.

SÉJOURNÉ, LAURETTE

1966 Arquitectura y Pintura en Teotihuacán. Siglo Veintiuno Editores, s.a., México.

SELER, EDUARD

1904 Wall Paintings at Mitla: A Mexican Picture Writing in Fresco. *In* Mexican and Central American Antiquities, Calendar Systems, and History. *Smithsonian Institution, Bureau of American Ethnology, Bulletin 28*, pp. 243–324. Washington.

SHARP, ROSEMARY

1970 Early Architectural Grecas in the Valley of Oaxaca. *Bulletin of Oaxaca Studies*, no. 32. Mitla.

1975 A Fine-Orange Vessel from the Olsen Collection. *Yale University Art Gallery Bulletin*, vol. 35, no. 2, pp. 8–23. New Haven.

1978 Architecture as Interelite Communication in Preconquest Oaxaca, Veracruz, and Yucatan. *In* Middle Classic Mesoamerica: A.D. 400–700 (Esther Pasztory, ed.), pp. 158–171. Columbia University Press, New York.

n.d.a Greca: An Exploratory Study of Relationships between Art, Society, and Personality. Unpublished dissertation. The University of North Carolina, Chapel Hill, 1972.

n.d.b Trading Chiefs to Warring Kings: The Political Nexus of Symbolic Forms during the Mesoamerican Epiclassic Period in Northern Yucatan. Paper delivered at the 42nd Annual Meeting, Society for American Archaeology, New Orleans (forthcoming).

n.d.c Feathered-Serpent Imagery in Northern Yucatan, Mexico: A Dialectical Approach. Paper presented before the Seminar on Pre-Columbian and

Primitive Art, Columbia University, New York, 1977.

n.d.d Pilgrims and Peddlers: Threshold Men in Postclassic Mexican Manuscripts. Unpublished manuscript.

SHEPARD, ANNA O.

1948 The Symmetry of Abstract Design, with Special Reference to Ceramic Decoration. *Carnegie Institution of Washington, Publication 547, Contributions to American Anthropology and History*, no. 47. Washington.

SPINDEN, HERBERT J.

1916 Portraiture in Central American Art. *In* Holmes Anniversary Volume: Anthropological Essays (F. W. Hodge, ed.), pp. 434–450. Washington.

1957 Maya Art and Civilization. The Falcon's Wing Press, Indian Hills.

STEPHENS, JOHN L.

1858 Incidents of Travel in Yucatan. 2 vols. Harper & Brothers, New York.

TAMBIAH, S. J.

1976 World Conqueror and World Renouncer: A Study of Buddhism and Polity in Thailand against a Historical Background. Cambridge University Press, Cambridge.

TELLO, JULIO C.

1960 Chavín: Cultura Matriz de la Civilización Andina, Primera Parte. Publicación Antropológica del Archivo "Julio C. Tello" de la Universidad Nacional Mayor de San Marcos, vol. II. Lima.

THOMPSON, J. ERIC S.

1934 Sky Bearers, Colors and Directions in Maya and Mexican Religion. *Carnegie Institution of Washington, Publication 436, Contributions to American Archaeology*, vol. II, no. 10, pp. 209–242. Washington.

1939 Las Llamadas "Fachadas de Quetzalcouatl." *In* Vigesimoséptimo Congreso Internacional de Americanistas, Actas de la Primera Sesión, Celebrada en la Ciudad de México en 1939, tomo I. México.

1952 The Introduction of Puuc Style of Dating at Yaxchilan. *Carnegie Institution of Washington, Department of Archaeology, Notes on Middle American Archaeology and Ethnology*, vol. IV, no. 110, pp. 196–202. Cambridge.

1958 Symbols, Glyphs, and Divinatory Almanacs for Diseases in the Maya Dresden and Madrid Codices. *American Antiquity*, vol. 23, no. 3, pp. 297–308.

1962 A Catalog of Maya Hieroglyphs. University of Oklahoma Press, Norman.

1966 The Rise and Fall of Maya Civilization. Second edition, enlarged. University of Oklahoma Press, Norman.

1970a Maya History and Religion. University of Oklahoma Press, Norman.

1970b The Bacabs: Their Portraits and Their Glyphs. *In* Monographs and Papers in Maya Archaeology (William R. Bullard, ed.), *Papers of the Peabody Museum of Archaeology and Ethnology, Harvard University*, vol. 61, pp. 469–487. Cambridge.

1972 A Commentary on the Dresden Codex: A Maya Hieroglyphic Book. *Memoirs of the American Philosophical Society*, vol. 93. Philadelphia.

1973a Maya Rulers of the Classic Period and the Divine Right of Kings. *In* The Iconography of Middle American Sculpture, pp. 52–71. The Metropolitan Museum of Art, New York.

1973b The Maya Glyph for Capture or Conquest and an Iconographic Representation of Itzam Na on Yucatecan Façades. *In* Studies in Ancient Mesoamerica (John Graham, ed.), *Contributions of the University of California Archaeological Research Facility*, no. 18, pp. 203–207. Berkeley.

1975 The Grolier Codex. *In* Studies in Ancient Mesoamerica, II (John Graham, ed.), *Contributions of the University of California Archaeological Research Facility*, no. 27, pp. 1–9. Berkeley.

TOZZER, ALFRED M.

1957 Chichen Itza and Its Cenote of Sacrifice: A Comparative Study of Contemporaneous Maya and Toltec. *Memoirs of the Peabody Museum of Archaeology and Ethnology, Harvard University*, vols. XI and XII. Cambridge.

TOZZER, ALFRED M. (ed.)

1941 Landa's Relación de las Cosas de Yucatan: A Translation. *Papers of the Peabody Museum of American Archaeology and Ethnology, Harvard University*, vol. XVIII. Cambridge.

TURNER, V. W.

1968 The Drums of Affliction: A Study of Religious Processes among the Ndembu of Zambia. Clarendon Press, Oxford, and the International African Institute.

WEBB, MALCOM C.

1978 The Significance of the "Epiclassic" Period in Mesoamerican Prehistory. *In* Cultural Continuity in Mesoamerica (David L. Browman, ed.), pp. 155–178. Mouton Publishers, The Hague.

WESTHEIM, PAUL

1965 The Art of Ancient Mexico. Doubleday and Company, Inc., Garden City.

WHEATLEY, PAUL
1971   The Pivot of the Four Quarters: A Preliminary
        Enquiry into the Origins and Character of the
        Ancient Chinese City. Aldine Publishing Com-
        pany, Chicago.

WILLEY, GORDON R.
1962   The Early Great Styles and the Rise of the Pre-
        Columbian Civilizations. *American Anthropolo-
        gist*, vol. 64, no. 1, pp. 1–14.

1973   Mesoamerican Art and Iconography and the In-
        tegrity of the Mesoamerican Ideological System.
        In The Iconography of Middle American Sculp-
        ture, pp. 153–162. The Metropolitan Museum
        of Art, New York.

1976   Mesoamerican Civilization and the Idea of
        Transcendence. *Antiquity*, vol. L, no. 1, pp.
        205–215.

1977   The Rise of Maya Civilization: A Summary
        View. *In* The Origins of Maya Civilization
        (Richard E. W. Adams, ed.), pp. 383–423.
        School of American Research, University of
        New Mexico Press, Albuquerque.

WILLEY, GORDON R., and DEMITRI B. SHIMKIN
1973   The Maya Collapse: A Summary View. *In* The
        Classic Maya Collapse (T. Patrick Culbert, ed.),
        pp. 457–491. School of American Research,
        University of New Mexico Press, Albuquerque.

WINTER, MARCUS, MARGARITA GAXIOLA, and
ADRIANA ALANIZ
1975   Secuencia Arqueológica del Valle de Oaxaca.
        Centro Regional de Oaxaca, Instituto Nacional
        de Antropología e Historia, Oaxaca.

ZIMMERMANN, GÜNTER
1956   Die Hieroglyphen der Maya-Handschriften.
        Cram, de Gruyter & Co., Hamburg.